■ *A FIRST ZEN READER*

D0285861

A First Zen Reader

COMPILED AND TRANSLATED BY

TREVOR LEGGETT

CHARLES E. TUTTLE COMPANY

Rutland, Vermont & Tokyo, Japan

Published by the Charles E. Tuttle Company, Inc.
of Rutland, Vermont & Tokyo, Japan
with editorial offices at
Suido 1-chome, 2-6, Bunkyo-ku, Tokyo

© 1960 by Charles E. Tuttle Company, Inc.

Library of Congress Catalog
Card No. 60-12739

International Standard Book No. 0-8048-0180-0

First edition, 1960
Nineteenth printing, 1990

Printed in Japan

Reverently dedicated to
THE LATE DR. HARI PRASAD SHASTRI,
Pandit and Jnani of India

■ CONTENTS

■ *ACKNOWLEDGEMENTS*

FOR PERMISSION to translate their books, I am deeply grateful to Primate Takashina and Abbot Amakuki; for instruction on Zen, to Primate Takashina and M. Takei (former head monk at Sojiji); for help with the translation, to Tsuji Somei of Engakuji and Professor Nishimura Shigeshi.

I owe a great debt to Mr. Takasaki Masami in study, in judo, and in life.

Some parts of the translations in this book have appeared in the British Vedanta magazine, *Self-Knowledge*.

T. L.

■ INTRODUCTION

THE ZEN sect of Buddhism claims to transmit the special realization attained by Shakyamuni Buddha in the meditation posture under the bodhi tree at Gaya, after six years of austere spiritual practices and at the end of a long meditation (six days and nights, in one tradition). This realization freed him from all sufferings and limitations for ever. It was handed on by him to his disciple Kashyapa, and thereafter in unbroken lines through patriarchs and teachers in India, China, Korea, and Japan, transmitted "from heart to heart" as might be passed on a bowl of water without a drop being spilled. In China the sect split into a number of different lines. After dominating Buddhism for centuries it is now in decay in China but still influential in Japan. The two main surviving transmissions there are the Rinzai, which is divided into a number of subsects, and the Soto, to which about two-thirds of the Japanese temples belong.

The Rinzai and Soto agree on the main points; they differ in the stress given to certain elements in Zen, notably what is called koan. This is a sort of riddle, not completely solvable by the intellect, which is an artificial method of concentrating the energies of a spiritual student. The koan method was devised quite late in Zen history. The Rinzai emphasizes concentration on koan, especially those in the anthologies *Hekiganroku* and *Mumonkan*. The Soto, though it has its own collection, the *Shoyoroku,* does not make so much of them, pointing out that the masters of the golden age of Zen in the T'ang dynasty did not rely on artificial koan. Mostly the koan are stories about these masters, though Hakuin (1685–1768) in 18th-century Japan devised one of the most famous, the "sound of one hand." Even this may derive from a phrase in the *Hekiganroku*.

The texts here translated will give a general idea of Zen theory and practice. Except for the two extracts contained in the "Bodhidharma and the Emperor," they are not technical Buddhist works but are for the layman. The backbone of the book is two series of lectures by two famous contemporary masters: Takashina Rosen, the present primate of the Soto sect and president of the Japan Buddhist Association, and Amakuki Sessan, a well-known master of the Rinzai sect.

The ordinary Japanese today has no deep knowledge of Buddhism, and these texts do not presuppose such knowledge. Here is a brief sketch of the Buddhist background of Zen for a reader who has never touched the subject. All the points are more fully explained in the body of the book, and the statements in this summary are not completely accurate.

The world of our experience is constantly changing; it is technically called Sansara, birth-and-death or life-and-death. Man instinctively seeks permanence in it, and so it is a constant source of suffering and disappointment to him. Our experience is, however, partly illusory. The illusion consists in taking as completely real the distinctions and limitations created by the mind. The truth of the world is Nirvana, absolutely free from distinctions and limitations, but because of ignorance *(avidya)* the mind experiences it as differentiated and limited. By the practice of Zen (literally "meditation" in Japanese) the confused, contrary, and upside-down notions can be discarded and Nirvana known directly. In Samadhi, the peak of meditation, distinctions vanish, and meditator and object of meditation are one.

Nirvana is beyond all definitions because it is beyond mind; it is hinted at in words like immortality, bliss, purity, and (true) selfhood. Inasmuch as a fundamental Buddhist doctrine is that things have no individual self, it is clear that selfhood does not here mean anything limited. In fact, all the terms are only provisional. Nirvana is sometimes called Sameness because it is free from all distinctions, and sometimes the Void because it is free from all conditions.

The Buddha is one who has realized that his nature is not a limited egoity but the conditionless Nirvana. Nirvana is therefore also called Buddha nature. All living beings have the Buddha nature. By practising morality, holy study, and meditation (Zen) they can awaken the wisdom *(prajna)* which realizes the true nature. Such realization or awakening is called in Japanese *satori*. It also has the sense of enlightenment. A Bodhisattva is one far advanced on the spiritual path to Buddhahood. Note, however, that the Buddha nature is already perfect within him as within all; the process is realization, not creation, of the Buddha.

There are devotional practices in some sects. Such are called "other power." For the relation of this to "self-power," see pages 117–18.

Mahayana means the Buddhism historically associated with northern India, China, Korea, Japan, Tibet, and Mongolia. It stresses the Bodhisattva ideal of helping all to attain realization, as against the Shravakas and Pratyeka Buddhas, who are said to strive for themselves alone. Mahayana has its own scriptures (sutras).

The last Sanskrit words to explain are *bodhi* and *karma*. Bodhi, literally "enlightenment," often means wisdom, the same as prajna. Karma means cause and effect extended to the psychological and moral realms; every detail of what happens to anybody is the result of his past actions, good following good, and evil following evil.

In these translations "heart" and "mind" generally stand for the same word in the original. This word is literally "heart" but by extension, as in English, it includes what we understand by "mind." I have preferred the translation as heart wherever possible, because for many people mind has a cerebral connotation. One form of Zen illness is caused by the vital energy rising uncontrolled to the head; the proper concentration is on the centre of the body. Zen master Hakuin puts extraordinary stress on this point; some meditation pictures by his disciple Torei show it diagrammatically. It is thus nearer Zen practice to speak of realizing the Buddha heart rather than the Buddha mind, at any rate for beginners.

Readers should note the special meaning of the word which has to be translated "original." On page 29 is explained the difference between realization-with-a-beginning and realization-from-the-beginning or original realization. In a similar sense should be understood such common Zen phrases as original mind, original face, original nature, and so on. If this point is grasped, many puzzles in Zen writing disappear. Related to it is the phrase "practice and realization are one." In the Zen of Buddhahood-from-the-beginning, practice is merely realization of the present fact of Buddhahood; practice is realization, not a means to create future realization of a future condition.

The Buddhism of India is not in every way the same as that of China, and again Japanese Buddhism has its own peculiarities. The differences are not small. However, the tradition is that teaching should be suited to the hearer as medicine to the patient, and the variations may be regarded as instances of Skilful Means or Hoben in Japanese. (It must be admitted that some great Japanese masters do not subscribe to the Hoben doctrine.)

Where the translated texts quote from Sanskrit or Chinese sources, I have translated according to my author's rendering, which may not be the only one possible. In some cases where he seems to quote, the author is paraphrasing or even varying the original text. Where the author gives a Chinese original followed by a free Japanese translation, only the latter is given.

Indian names are given in an approximation to the original; such names as Shakyamuni and Ananda are familiar to the West. Most Chinese names and words are given in the way Japanese pronounce them; e.g., Rinzai and not Linchi. This may be distressing to Chinese scholars, but it seems likely that most of the material on Zen in the future will come from Japan, and a choice must be made. There is nothing sacred in the modern Mandarin pronunciation, particularly in the confusing transliteration generally adopted. The famous negative monosyllable uttered by Joshu, in reply to the question whether there is Buddha nature in the dog, is now pronounced in the Chinese standard language "wu." But the Japanese pronunciation "mu" is nearer to Joshu's T'ang dynasty pronunciation. I am not quite consistent, for I keep such Chinese words as T'ang and Sung for the dynasties on the ground that we know them, and that they are not Zen terms or names.

I have not indicated the long vowels in Japanese. The common words and names will no doubt be anglicized, just as judo and tycoon have been. Experience shows that the English language will not retain for long diacritical marks attached to foreign words. Japanese names are given with the surname first; e.g., in the name Oka Kyugaku, the family name is Oka, and Kyugaku is the Buddhist (what we automatically tend to call the Christian) name.

There are numerous allusions in Zen literature, some Buddhist and some to customs, history, or literature in general. For instance, the reply of Soji to Bodhidharma *(see page 112)*: "It is as when Ananda had a vision of the paradise of the Buddha of the East; it appeared and then vanished," does not mean a failure of vision. It refers to a sutra in which the Buddha creates for his disciple Ananda an appearance of the paradise in the room where they are, and when the Buddha withdraws his magic power the vision vanishes. I have translated it in this sense. To catch such allusions the student may read books on Buddhism in general; those by Dr. E. Conze can be recommended. Many of the Zen allusions will be found somewhere in the works of Dr. D. Suzuki. Inevitably some overtones will be missed. In Chinese poetry white clouds often stand for spiritual contemplation and experience *(see page 108)*. The dark rain clouds of worldly success soon vanish, but the sky is never without the high white clouds. Again, a novice in anything is associated with the colour white and an expert with black, so the "white-robed" in the Case of the White Hare *(see page 57)* has the connotation of a spiritual beginner.

In some cases where the whole point depends on a verbal play, or on an allusion cumbersome to explain, I have omitted the passage. I have also left out some pages in the "Song of Meditation" book where the author issues a warning to his countrymen, then on the brink of plunging into a disastrous war.

The texts here translated are not systematic expositions. The sentences and paragraphs are thrusts designed to awaken the sleeping prajna wisdom. When it wakes, the Buddha nature is recognized, which is from the beginning ever perfect in enlightenment and realization. This, and not discussion, is the aim of the authors.

The Original Face

Face

A SERMON BY DAITO KOKUSHI

"THE ORIGINAL FACE" is a sermon delivered to the Empress Hanazono by Zen master Myocho, who is best known under the name bestowed upon him by the emperor: Daito Kokushi. Kokushi means literally *"teacher of the nation."* Daito (1281–1337) was one of the great lights of the Rinzai sect in Japan. He hid himself for some time, disguised as a beggar, to evade fame. The picture by Hakuin (Plate 1) shows him in this role.

■ THE ORIGINAL FACE

ALL ZEN students should devote themselves at the beginning to *zazen* (sitting in meditation). Sitting in either the fully locked position or the half-locked position, with the eyes half-shut, see the original face which was before father or mother was born. This means to see the state before the parents were born, before heaven and earth were parted, before you received human form. What is called the original face will appear. That original face is something without colour or form, like the empty sky in whose clarity there is no form.

The original face is really nameless, but it is indicated by such terms as original face, the Lord, the Buddha nature, and the true Buddha. It is as with man, who has no name at birth, but afterwards various names are attached to him. The seventeen hundred koan or themes to which Zen students devote themselves are all only for making them see their original face. The World-honoured One sat in meditation in the snowy mountains for six years, then saw the morning star and was enlightened, and this was seeing his original face. When it is said of others of the ancients that they had a great realization, or a great breaking-through, it means they saw the original face. The Second Patriarch stood in the snow and cut off his arm to get realization; the Sixth Patriarch heard the phrase from the Diamond Sutra and was enlightened. Reiun was enlightened when he saw the peach blossoms, Kyogen on hearing the tile hit the bamboo, Rinzai when struck by Obaku, Tozan on seeing his own reflection in the water.

All this is what is called "meeting the lord and master."

The body is a house, and it must have a master. It is the master of the house who is known as the original face. Experiencing heat and cold and so on, or feeling a lack, or having desires—these are all delusive thoughts and do not belong to the true master of the house. These delusive thoughts are something added. They are things which vanish with each breath. To be dragged along by them is to fall into hell, to circle in the six paths of reincarnation. By going deeper and deeper into zazen, find the source of the thoughts. A thought is something without any form or body, but owing to the conviction of those thoughts remaining even after death, man falls into hell with its many pains, or suffers in the round of this changing world.

Every time a thought arises, throw it away. Just devote yourself to sweeping away the thoughts. Sweeping away thoughts means performing zazen. When thought is put down, the original face appears. The thoughts are like clouds; when the clouds have cleared, the moon appears. That moon of eternal truth is the original face.

The heart itself is verily the Buddha. What is called "seeing one's nature" means to realize the heart Buddha. Again and again put down the thoughts, and then see the heart Buddha. It might be supposed from this that the true nature will not be visible except when sitting in meditation. That is a mistake. Yoka Daishi says: "Going too is Zen; sitting too is Zen. Speaking or silent, moving the body or still, he is at peace." This teaches that going and sitting and talking are all Zen. It is not only being in zazen and suppressing the thoughts. Whether rising or sitting, keep concentrated and watchful. All of a sudden, the original face will confront you.

1 (opposite). DAITO KOKUSHI, BY HAKUIN.
Daito, who spent some years as a beggar to escape spiritual fame, is here shown in this role. The poem refers to an incident when he was recognized. Note the difference between the calligraphy here and that of Plate 5, in which Hakuin writes of himself. (See page 20.)

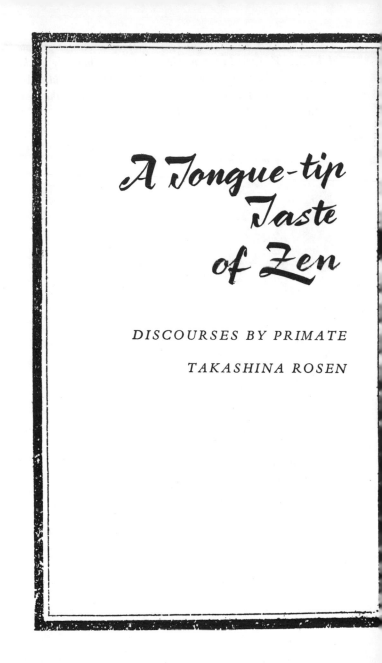

A Tongue-tip Taste of Zen

DISCOURSES BY PRIMATE

TAKASHINA ROSEN

TAKASHINA Rosen (Plate 2, below) *is* kancho *or primate of the Soto Zen sect in Japan. He is reverenced not only by the followers of this sect; as president of the Japan Buddhist Association he is looked up to by the other sects as one of the great Buddhist figures of present-day Japan.*

Zetto Zemmi *or* A Tongue-tip Taste of Zen *is a collection of his discourses on Zen, and can be taken as an authoritative exposition by a very eminent contemporary Zen master.*

2. TAKASHINA ROSEN.
This photograph, taken in 1958, shows the primate of the Soto Zen sect in meditation posture.

■ CHAPTER ONE

WHAT I AM going to say about Zen is not an adaptation of formal lectures, but intended as a talk to people who wish to have a correct knowledge of Zen and to understand it. The influence exerted on Japanese life by Zen doctrines and spirit is very great. The *miso* soup, *takuan* pickled radish, *tofu* beancurd, and other things which are the mainstay of our people's daily diet have almost all come from Zen. The rule of washing the face and rinsing the mouth every morning without fail was laid down by Zen master Dogen in the 13th century. The arts of the tea ceremony and flower arrangement have the Zen spirit at the root of their formal development. Yet if asked what Zen is, to reply is very difficult. Nevertheless it is hoped that beginners can get from this book a little understanding of it.

Zen master Dogen says in his *Shobo Genzo* classic that practising Zen means zazen or sitting in meditation. Originally the word Zen (meditation) was an abbreviation for zazen, the syllable *za* having later gradually dropped out. The same classic says: "Zazen is the front portal of Buddhism." To enter the inner halls of Buddhism it is proper to go through the front portal. It may seem easier to slip in through a back door, but only when entering by the front with the proper ceremony can we be accepted by the family and know them. Once we know the family we are free to go in by the back door or side door without formality, and it will cause no disturbance to the household.

Buddhism was introduced into Japan in the time of the Emperor Kimmei in the 6th century, but it was only some Buddha images and copies of sutras that came, and not yet the real Buddhism. In the 13th century the patriarch Dogen went to Mount Tendo in China, where he became a disciple of Zen master Nyojo. He "loosed and dropped off body and mind," and, thus released, returned home, bringing the true tradition of zazen.

The most important thing in connection with zazen—its real meaning as taught by Dogen—is often misunderstood. Some think that zazen is practised to obtain satori (realization), and that when satori is complete, zazen is no longer needed. This is the Zen of "awaiting satori" and it has a somewhat different flavour from the Zen where zazen is itself the Buddha action. In the former, zazen is practised in the spirit of hoping for realization, and only up to that point; after satori, zazen is not regarded as important. But Zen master Dogen stresses that the true way and true tradition of the Buddhas and patriarchs is to sit in meditation for its own sake, and not merely as a means to an expected satori. It is true that when concentrating on a koan, the whole life has to be thrown into the practice with satori as the aim. But the traditional zazen of the Buddhas and patriarchs is what is called the Samadhi of the Buddha-in-his-own-glory, and not at all zazen practised as a means to satori. In the zazen posture the glory of the Buddhas and patriarchs is manifest; it is the Buddha action and the Buddha way. The great patriarch Dogen stresses this point. Zazen is the state where the Buddhas are in their own glory. The three actions of body, speech, and mind are impressed with the seal of Buddhahood and manifest the Buddhas. Soto Zen is the pure meditation in the seated posture, the zazen always practised by the Buddhas and patriarchs, and therefore it is continued even after satori. It is not that realization is unnecessary, but they are mistaken who think that Zen is just something to be practised till they scrape through to satori, and then to be dropped.

The traditional Way is eternal, and so zazen too is eternal. It is the Buddha action pervading all life and all the worlds.

In the East, meditation power has flourished in the world as the basis of civilization, and it has invigorated science, art, technology, economics, and all branches of culture. And so it is said that, in our zazen, practice is not different from realization. In the actual practice, there is the satori in that time and that place, and furthermore both are eternal.

In Japan today there are generally said to be three main sects, the Obaku, the Rinzai, and the Soto. The Obaku sect has its headquarters at Uji. Perhaps because there is such a strong Chinese influence in it, this sect did not develop in Japan, and it has only a few temples. The Rinzai sect is divided into a number of subsects, with head temples at Kyoto, Kamakura, and elsewhere. It has had great influence in the development of literature and art. In its method of zazen the important thing is passing through koan, so that it is called the Zen of awaiting realization. The koan are meditated upon one after another, and stages of satori are attained, koan by koan, like mounting the rungs of a ladder. In this view, it is only after the point of realization that Buddhahood comes into existence. The Soto sect has two head temples and fifteen thousand branch temples, and the sect is not split. The Zen is called "silent illumination" as against the school of "awaiting realization"; the teaching is pure meditation, and the non-difference of practice and realization. Our zazen is sitting with the Buddha seal manifest on body, speech, and mind, and this zazen is the Buddha action. Such is the realization-practice of Zen master Dogen, the uttermost depths of wisdom.

In zazen, as it is said, there is reading the scriptures, performance of duties, taking tea, and taking rice. As against the view that Buddhahood begins only after satori, which is the Zen of realization-with-a-beginning, this is the Zen of realization-from-the-beginning. Zazen is the Buddha action of the self which is a Buddha from the very beginning, and so throughout life it never ceases. It is a zazen which manifests realization-from-the-beginning or original realization. Thus the same zazen varies among the sects, and we should be clear about it. Each view has its own advantages, and this is not a matter for carping criticism.

Of the greatness of the merit of this zazen, Dogen says: "If all the Buddhas of the ten directions, countless as the grains of sand of the holy river, were to put out all their strength, and by their Buddha wisdom seek to measure the merit of a man in meditation, never could they even approach it."

Nevertheless, it can easily happen that as meditation power increases with practice, a Zen illness of pride in zazen arises. Normally we are submerged in the thousand confusions of the world, whirled round in the innumerable shifts and changes of life. As a result it becomes very easy to be caught up in things, and then those who wish to release themselves and be free throw themselves into zazen. But as the sitting becomes a major part of their life, they now get caught in the Zen illness. When concentration becomes one-pointed, in their meditation a Buddha appears, or demons or gods; perhaps they feel encircled by a snake, or other phenomena appear. Now all these things, even if it is the Buddha himself who appears to welcome us, are only the Zen illness. They are aberrations of zazen. One thing we have to note very carefully. It is that even if a man sees the Buddha's form so clearly that he is convinced it is the Buddha, or if he is pursued by a devil-mask and so feels fear, this is all the realm of ghosts and no more.

■ CHAPTER TWO

FOR THE serious student, posture is the first step in zazen or sitting in meditation. It is a peculiar fact that for spiritual practice, first of all the posture of the body must be made just right, whereas in physical training we always have to make sure that it is approached in the proper "sporting" spirit, getting that right first. In zazen, then, we have to see that the body is in the posture laid down as correct. Zen master Dogen, in the *Fukan Zazen-gi* classic on meditation, gives full details.

As to place, a thick mat is spread, the small round meditation cushion put on it, and the seat taken on that. If there is no meditation cushion, an ordinary cushion doubled over may be used. The rear half of the buttocks is placed on the cushion, and the seat made firm *(Plate 3a)*. There are two main postures, the fully locked and the half-locked positions. The names refer to the placing of the legs. In the first the legs are locked together by first setting the right foot on the left thigh and then bringing the left foot over onto the right thigh *(Plate 3b)*. The right hand, palm upward, is laid on the left foot, and the left hand, also palm upward, on the right hand. The tips of the thumbnails are to be touching. The spine is quite straight and erect, neither inclined to the left nor leaning to the right, neither bending forward nor falling back, but with ears in line with the shoulders and the nose above the navel *(Plate 3c)*. Such is the correct meditation posture. The tongue touches the upper jaw, the mouth is closed, and the eyes slightly opened. The breathing should be natural, but so that the breath as

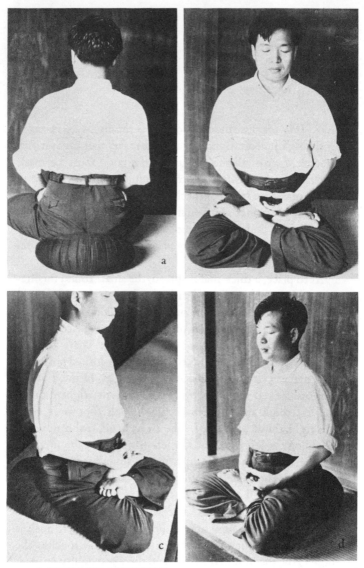

3. SITTING FOR MEDITATION.

A student at the Sojiji Monastery, near Tokyo, demonstrates the proper postures for *zazen*. (See pages 31 and 33.)

it passes through the nostrils is barely audible. In this way the body is settled for meditation.

The half-locked position is putting just the left foot on the right thigh *(Plate 3d)*. However, as a change, the left foot can be taken down and the right foot put on the left thigh. The *Zazen-gi* only mentions the position with the left foot on the right thigh, but for students either position, namely with just one foot on the opposite thigh, can be taken as the half-locked position. The other points are the same as in the fully locked posture.

Beginners may use the half-locked position first and slowly progress to the fully locked. Those who always wear Western clothes and sit in chairs find the fully locked position difficult, and they may sit on their feet in the Japanese way, or it is also permissible to sit for meditation on a chair. People should select the position they can manage.

The ancient classification of human posture is into four: walking, standing, sitting, and lying. It may be asked why the Zen rule prescribes only sitting. On this the Patriarch Dogen says: "Of the four, why is the sitting posture alone given as appropriate for meditation and realization? Know then that from ancient times all the Buddhas have followed this practice as the path to enter satori. To the request for a reason, let it merely be known that the reason is that this is the way of the Buddhas, and one should not ask further. The patriarchs praise it as the gateway to peace and bliss. This is not the way of practice of only one Buddha or two Buddhas, but the path of all the Buddhas and all the patriarchs."

For one who has realized and is in the Samadhi of Buddha-in-his-own-glory, there is no necessity to stick to going or standing or sitting or lying exclusively, but in general the correct sitting posture, the fully locked position, is the right way—so we are told by generations of patriarchs and teachers of the past who followed the example of Shakyamuni Buddha and have left a record of their own experience.

■ CHAPTER THREE

WHAT WAS it that Buddha wished to teach? Was it sagacity? Was it brilliant academic understanding? Was his aim to encourage the reading of the sutras, or asceticism or austerities? In reality it was none of these. He simply wished to show all living beings how to set in right order the body and mind. The method of doing this is given in the classic on meditation called *Zazen-gi:* "Think the unthinkable. How to think the unthinkable? Be without thoughts—this is the secret of meditation." Being without thoughts is the object of Zen meditation; the control of body and mind is only a method of reaching it. When body and mind are controlled, from the ensuing absence of thoughts are born spontaneously brilliant understanding, perfect Buddha-wisdom, reading of the sutras and devotion, asceticism, and austerities. There are some who have too hastily assumed that holy reading, devotion, or austerities have a value in themselves, but this is not the traditional Zen as handed down through the great master Dogen.

What is meant by absence of thoughts? The living Samadhi of all the Buddhas is no other than that state of absence of thoughts. Taking the words literally, one might think it meant to be like a tree or a stone, but it is not that at all. It cannot be understood by our ordinary consciousness, but neither shall we get it by unconsciousness. We can only grasp it by experiencing it in ourselves.

Beginners, when they first hear that the secret of Zen is to be without thoughts but that it is not attained by consciousness or by unconsciousness, cannot understand at all what it can be, and are bewildered. Now instead of wondering how to get it, or trying to understand it or to analyze it, the essential thing is to take a resolute plunge into death, to give up one's body and life itself. It means to cut off all our discriminating fancies at the root and source. If we go on cutting them off at the root, then of itself the freedom from thought will come, which means that our original realization appears, and this is called satori. An ancient says: "In Zen the important thing is to stop the course of the mind." It means to stop the workings of our empirical consciousness, the mass of thoughts, ideas, and perceptions. Great Dogen says: "Cut off thought by the power of meditation. By this alone nearly everyone can attain the Way." Attaining the Way is realizing the Buddha heart which is our own true nature. The radiance of the Buddha heart breaks forth from ourselves; the compassion of the Buddha flows out of the Buddha heart within us. We come to know that the majesty of Buddha is the majesty of our self also.

The doctrine of karma is one aspect of Buddhism. In this doctrine, the whole phenomenal universe as perceived by us is understood to be an effect, corresponding to the previous thoughts, speech, and actions of the individual and of all living beings, which are the cause. In fact the whole phenomenal universe is experienced according to our karma. The three forms of karma, namely action of body, speech, and thought, can all be embraced under the heading of actions of the mind or heart. Whether this heart is the Buddha heart or not is the cause which determines good or evil for us. And if we only stress our ego and do not cut off the thoughts, the Buddha heart does not manifest.

The real difficulty of Zen meditation is how to stop the course of the mind, how to cut off thought. Some twenty-five hundred years ago at Kushinara in India, the World-honoured One, Shakyamuni Buddha, was about to die. In the final teachings to his disciples, the last phrase of the instructions about mind and senses is: "You must subjugate the mind." This does not mean the Buddha mind or Buddha heart, but it means the egoistic heart of the ordinary man who employs his mind actively all the time. Was there ever any chameleon comparable to the human heart? Just now it was happy and laughing, but now all at once it is sad, then in a rage about something or other; or it wants to eat, or to sleep, to praise or to slander. In so-called women's gossip the confusions of the mind become noisily apparent as speech. And so far it may not be so bad, but then there also spring up terrible things: robbery and murder—all transformations of the egoistic heart. This is why in the Vijnanavada (Consciousness Only) school of Buddhism all changes are called transformations of consciousness.

As to whether the heart in itself is good or bad, some say good and some say bad, and there was also a view among the ancients that it is neither. However it may be, what is clear is that our minds from morning to evening in their ceaseless activity undergo thousands and millions of changes and transformations, good and bad. Reason and morality tell us to take every possible care that we do not slip into a wrong path, but instead strive to keep the carriage of our life on the right road. An old poet sings: "When you feel it pulling, do not loose the reins of the colt of the heart, which would enter the evil paths," and again: "In the cooking-pot of the world, cook well and not badly; the human heart is the free-moving ladle." According to how the free ladle is lifted and lowered, the things are cooked well or badly. The human heart is likewise fundamentally free. They say that it is important all the time to give attention to the right path, but Zen does not speak of morality in quite this way. It is just a question of the Buddha heart, which prompts us to take a step beyond, to end the coursing of the mind, to cut off the thought. Once and for all, we have to cut off the working of the mind, which is the inner ego from which the evil emerges.

Buddhism teaches that the human heart has two aspects: the pure heart and the impure heart. But the heart in itself is not two; it is only classified in these two ways according to its workings. The pure heart is the pure heart of our own nature, our natural heart which is not a whit different from the Buddha heart. Opposed to this is the impure heart which gives us no peace from morning till night, the egoistic heart of illusions, the passion-ridden heart. Because the selfish, passionate heart is not natural, we are always afflicted with sufferings; endlessly this heart, absolutely reckless, leads men astray.

Fundamentally our true heart, our true nature, is pure and infinite, like the moon clear in the blue sky. At some distant time past our knowing, it was tainted by passion and became the impure heart, something not our real self but which came afterwards. This which came afterwards becomes predominant and sets at naught the true heart, just as the concubine sets at naught the real wife. How often one has read in the papers that the steward of some large estate, or the manager of a great firm perhaps, has set at naught his masters and, using the money for himself, has brought ruin all around. Just in this way we entrust ourselves to the operations of the deluded and passion-ridden heart, so that the real master, the Buddha heart, cannot even show its face. The thoughts of the impure heart are topsyturvy, for it sees reality as upside down. The villains who act as chief contributors to the delusion are what the Buddha called "the brigands of the five senses." These five—eye, ear, nose, tongue, and body—take in all the tempting objects and convey them to the impure heart in order to satisfy it. For this reason they are technically called roots, because just in this way the roots of a tree convey the sap to the branches and leaves to satisfy them. Of course the mischievous operation of the senses is not natural; their true working is not wrong. But the impure heart misuses them and only lets them work in wrong directions. As it is said in the Buddha's last teachings, "these five take the heart as their master." So the wicked nature of the impure heart is compared to a venomous serpent or a wild beast. It bears off the life which should develop into the Buddha who is our true nature. In our breast is coiled the poisonous serpent which is always breathing out the fire of the three poisons, bringing on us agonies and sufferings.

To drive out the devilish impure heart and enable the pure radiance to shine from the pure heart within us, the five senses have to be cut off. And hence it is said that we should cut off thought. How are we to do it? There are several methods, but the Zen method is to sit in the meditation posture and swell with our breath and vitality what is called "the field of the elixir" (the abdomen below the navel). In this way the whole frame is invigorated. Then we meditate, discarding body and mind. Now the delusions which are the impure heart come up without ceasing. We should make these fancies, coming one after another, the koan (theme) of our meditation. What, after all, is this thought? Where did it come from? We penetrate with the spear-point of our meditation to the source of the successive fancies.

When we practise sitting in this way regularly and make progress in meditation, then of itself the meditation becomes deeper and fuller until there is no room for the fancies to show their heads. The practice is quite unrestricted, and the entry into the experience of truth is also unrestricted; in the end appears the glory of the true self, where the practice *is* the realization. This is called seeing one's true face, and it is said that nine out of ten people can achieve it (in this very life). The practice as described has nothing artificial about it, but its easiness is deceptive, and the old masters all had a hard time with it. There are many sayings about this, such as, "After winning a hundred battles, now I grow old in the great peace," or "How many times for your sake do I enter the green dragon's cave where the jewel is hidden!"

There is another method. First in the same way filling

the whole body with vigour, we wrestle with a koan which the teacher gives us. The "not" of Master Joshu, the "tree in the fore-court," the "true face," the "sound of one hand"—any of them will do. It is a question of using the koan to practise meditation with all the force of our will, one-pointedly and without distraction. If there is the least little bit of discriminating in this meditation, it will fail completely. Suppose, for instance, we are meditating on the sound of one hand. Though we try to understand it with the discriminating intellect, it will never be understood. We may think that we have understood, but this is no more than an understanding with the discriminating impure mind, which thinks "I" and "my" and "I do it." Zen meditation means to cut off at the root the mind which thinks "I understand it," and to enter the state where there is no impure discrimination; and one who rests satisfied at the stage of intellectual understanding is far from the goal of Zen. We are told to hear the sound of one hand, which alone cannot make a sound, and discrimination or analysis obviously cannot understand it. The essential thing is that the whole body and mind should be absorbed in the koan and no other thought should be able to arise, so that not only at the time of meditation but also in standing and walking and sitting and lying the meditation continues without a break. Then all unknown the power of the meditation matures. Abbot Reiun, seeing the peach flowers, became enlightened, and Zen master Kyogen at hearing the crack of a bamboo. In the way our karma may direct, heaven and earth are split open in an instant; as if a sluice had been opened, suddenly we attain bliss and life infinite.

Such was the realization of the old masters, and of this the *Zazen-gi* classic says: "Loosing and dropping off body and mind, your original face is clear before you." But there must not be any relaxation of attention; if there is even a slight wavering, the karma does not ripen into the psychological moment, any more than in the case of a dead man.

It is sufficient to penetrate completely into one koan. The great Realization is once for all; if there had to be a repetition, it would not have been complete satori. Of course there is nothing against a man examining all the seventeen hundred koan which exist, in order to try the power of his vision of the true self, but it does not mean that he has to solve more than one in order to be enlightened. If in the way described one presses on with burning faith, throwing one's whole power into the meditation, then it is absolutely certain that the time will come when he enters the living Samadhi of all the Buddhas. To adopt the method of koan is called the Zen of "awaiting satori." But in Soto Zen, the practice is just realizing; we meditate earnestly as the Buddha himself did, and it is not a question of wrestling with the koan and waiting for satori. We should understand the value of this practice of earnest sitting in meditation, which is the most important thing in the mental training leading to our real good, namely bringing out the Buddha light from our humanity. If it is done, then naturally through the Buddha heart our human nature is elevated. There is no distinction here of sharp or dull or clever or stupid. It is a fact that anyone, if he devotes himself wholeheartedly to spiritual meditation without wavering, reaches the supreme state.

■ CHAPTER FOUR

WHAT IS the aim of religion, and what is its *raison d'être?* People with a modern education clearly seem to be in doubt as to the answers. The trend of religion most obvious in society (particularly that of the so-called Revivalist sects) is chiefly towards healing, fortune-telling, and rituals. These are made out to be the very essence of religion. Such things are, it is true, phenomena associated with religion, but they are not its essence. Mere alleviation of sickness and misfortune, absurd dreams of wealth and success—if to realize these is true religion, then it is indeed opium.

The real religious quest is never on the plane of fulfilling such empirical desires. It is to penetrate deeply into daily life, into the world before us, and to seek practical experience of the life of Reality. This we call the heart of religion. When we think over everyday life, we see that it is founded on a great contradiction, and that our self-existence does not rest on any sure and firm foundation. As we realize the vanity of the world and understand the deep sinfulness of our ordinary conduct, for the first time arises the desire for the world of truth, of liberation, of unsullied purity. This is the manifesting of the religious spirit, and now the world of religion opens to us. But even when we do see the impermanence in our daily life, and the uncertainty of our self-existence, are we really awake to the contradiction in it? Of course intellectually we may be aware of it, but not deeply. We may feel the contradiction in a way, but there is after all quite a bit of self-deception in the ordinary man's life. (Which is why from the religious standpoint the world and the life of the world are called "lies.")

He who truly wakes to the impermanence and contradiction of the world is for the first time really awake. But the one who cannot in daily life see the self which is his true nature, whose interests are vulgar crazes and the things of the world, whose thought never leaves the circle of gossip and public opinion, whose desires are just for empirical happiness, material things, fame and gain—where is his true nature? In the viciousness called the world he has buried it; he has entombed the self.

Not understanding that everything is passing, thinking that old age, sickness, and death, which are the lot of all, are things that happen to other people, and deluding himself that somehow he will live for ever, passing his time in pursuit of name and profit and forgetting the real spirit of man, he has no serenity or philosophy. In this world governed by delusion and passion, religion does not exist, and in such a daily life the soul is broken. But from that very breaking, for the first time spiritual thoughts arise. He begins to reflect truly, and to seek a world where his self can live. About this, Zen master Dogen says: "What is called learning the way is learning the self," and again: "What is called learning the self is forgetting the self." Self-forgetfulness means to liberate the true self from the imprisoning ego. The word *gedatsu* (liberation) is composed of two Chinese characters, "to be loosed" and "to escape," and so it means literally to come out of bondage and to have freedom. The bondage may be either physical or spiritual. There are people who are in bondage to duties or to their feelings; there are those who weep under the burden of things which do not matter at all, those who, binding the mind by the mind, cannot rise from the depths. Everyone has heard about neurosis and hysteria and so on. Modern medicine tells us that in a great percentage of the cases the cause of illness is psychological, the binding of the self by the self. The point is that to be caught, whether by facts, fancies, dreams, or illusions, is equally imprisonment. The bondage appears in innumerable forms, but the chief of them, the bond which is their source, is the problem of life and death. The other minor problems just appear in the interval between birth and death. To this great fundamental problem the teaching of the Buddha offers a solution, ensuring us supreme peace. That state of great peace is called Nirvana, and it is a state in which there is identification with the Reality which is neither life nor death. Then is realized the world of divine compassion and peace. That Nirvana transcending life and death is universal Life, and the Life of our own immortality. In that Life appears and vanishes the bondage of birth-and-death, our individual life of less than a hundred years, all taken up with trivial worries. For the average man it is pain and sorrow. Who then is the villain of the piece? Who brings upon us the agony of imprisonment by the things of life and death? It is egoity; it is selfishness. Egoity always finds the excuses for us, never looks beyond external actions, always tries to fulfil the desire for the welfare of this little body alone. The body, which from the universal point of view exists for but an instant, wants against all reason to cling to life for ever. The universal Life pervades time and space without limit, but egoity sticks only to the life of one single body, and sets itself up against the great Life which is infinite.

Suppose, as an illustration, that a shade is put over the great lamp in the main hall of the temple. Now the range of its beams is restricted to a narrow area. This is like our human life—a tiny thing when compared with the great Life. But since it is fundamentally just a manifestation of that Life, by nature it seeks ultimately to become one with the great Life of Nirvana. If that Life is restricted by the shade of egoity, it becomes quite a small thing, and is bound, dissatisfied, tormented, and in agony. It is imprisoned in all kinds of limitations. The imprisonment is felt as if imposed from outside, but the truth is that there are no chains, and it is imposed by the self; the self suffers, imprisoned by itself. And as when the shade is removed, the rays of light suddenly illumine the whole hall, so the self of this present little life becomes, without changing, one with the great Life of Nirvana, and is able to experience the eternal reality. This is called the life of non-egoity *(muga)*, or the life of Buddha. Zazen has the power to bring us directly into the eternal life of non-egoity. When that power is matured, the distinctions between object and subject are transcended. That and I, I and that, become the Absolute, and now the hidden springs of action are released. The truth beyond everyday experience, purity beyond all passion, is revealed. This is the world of truth; it is reality beyond all the distinctions created by human individuality. Here the opposition of right and wrong, good and bad, beautiful and ugly, pleasant and hateful, enemy and friend, is annihilated, and there is a state of perfect Absoluteness. Thence is born the power to create a perfect and refined culture; in learning, art, economics, and everything else there will be developments embodying truth and reality. It will bring real prosperity to men. It is the religious glory of Buddhism and the essence of Zen, which is the core of Buddhism, to discover that power.

CHAPTER FIVE

IN WESTERN philosophy and theology there are various theories about the existence of God, and attempts are made to prove His existence. Leaving aside the rightness or wrongness of the arguments and the whole question of whether there is a God-in-heaven, what is certain is that He has not been seen with any physical eyes. In Buddhism, when the eye of the heart is opened and the universe viewed, the Buddha is everywhere. To Shakyamuni at the moment of enlightenment, things animate and inanimate, all together became the Truth: grass, trees, and earth—all, all, became Buddhas. In all the phenomena of the world the Buddha spirit is active. The courses of the sun, the moon, and the other heavenly bodies, the cycle of the seasons, in the spring the willows and flowers and in the autumn the red maple leaves and the clear moon—every year it is so and will doubtless go on for ten million years unchanged. In that regularity there is no disorder, and we cannot suppose that a universe which displays such regularity can be just in movement to no purpose. We can observe a purpose to which the spiritual activity is moving. There is a progress, there is a development, and it is the process by which all become Buddhas. This supreme goal the philosophers call truth, call the Absolute, call reality. Because its being is a mystery it is also called God, but different from the God-in-heaven worshipped by Christians and others. We can indicate it as the spiritual essence of the universe, the great Life of all. This is what Buddhism means by Buddha. It is not the manifest physical body which came to birth in India and passed away at the age of eighty, but the Buddha of the truth-body, truth without form, the Absolute, the spirit that pervades the whole universe. The Kegon Sutra says:

> *The Buddha pure and like space,*
> *Without shape or form pervades all.*

The Buddha body eternally fills all the worlds; it is the spiritual force in all phenomena everywhere. In plants and animals and minerals the Buddha light is shining forth, from the worlds countless as the sands, from every speck of dust, from all beings and things.

The Buddhist doctrine of the Buddha body teaches that it has three aspects: the *dharma* body or body of truth, the body of bliss, and the manifest physical body. The body of truth, as has been said, is the formless spiritual essence of all things. It is consciousness absolute, filling the universes with beginningless, endless, and infinite life. Its wonder is called God, and the word God means that wonder.

Next the body of bliss, which has a beginning but no end. When Shakyamuni on December 8th saw the morning star, his satori began, and the life of the satori never ends. It is distinct from the life of his physical body. Shakyamuni Buddha (we leave for the moment the question of his predecessors) handed it on to Kashyapa, he to Ananda, and he to Shanavasu, and I stand as ninety-third in the line of transmission through Bodhidharma, Nyojo, and Dogen. Hereafter the succession will continue unbroken without end. The form of this Buddha body is not the physical form of Shakyamuni. It has no form but is the life of the transmission of Shakyamuni, Bodhidharma, and Rosen. What is transmitted is a current by virtue of which is handed on the living realization, the fruit of the spiritual practices of Shakyamuni, and it cannot be seen by the physical eye as it is without colour or form. In other words, receiving the spiritual practices as the spirit of Shakyamuni's satori, the patriarchs and teachers, generation after generation, live the life of Zen, practising zazen. This is the bliss-body of

Shakyamuni the Enlightened One. The idea of the Western Paradise of Amitabha Buddha expresses the same truth.

The life and action in which flowed that spirit of Buddha produced Buddhist culture and passed it on. In the Japanese No drama, for instance, there was an actor called Hosho Kuro, and as is the custom, his chief pupil and successor took his name, which has been passed on for ten generations. The spirit of Hosho Kuro had a beginning but did not end with the first generation, being passed on to the second and third generations of pupils and so on, and they were each called Hosho Kuro. But the physical form of the present-day Hosho Kuro is not that of the first one.

So the life is transmitted. Now as to the manifest body of Buddha, this is a physical body, like that of Shakyamuni in India, which appears in a form appropriate to the natures of the people. In the *Shushogi* classic of Dogen, it is said that this was a human being in India like other human beings, whose satori was at thirty and whose passing away was at eighty.

There are, then, these three—the body of truth, the body of bliss, and the manifest physical body. In Japanese religious history the central role has been accorded to the bliss-body, which, manifesting through physical bodies all through human history, helps humanity and is revered as the living Buddha of the time. This is the beauty of the tradition as transmitted in Japan. The glory of Japanese culture has been based on the fact that it could show that Shakyamuni was not simply a man who lived and died, but that there was a handing on from one generation to the next and then to the next.

As to the supreme truth of the dharma body at the centre, it is the life essence pervading conscious and unconscious, and is instanced by Tozan's famous answer to the monk who asked him about the Buddha: "three pounds of linen." In this reply of Tozan we see how the Buddha of the Truth is ever manifest, radiating the Buddha light and in activity, whereas when the monk says "Buddha" he takes it as something glorious and set apart from ordinary living beings which are inglorious. He forgets that the self is from the beginning the Buddha of the Truth, and seeks a Buddha in another. But to forget self and seek Buddha in others is after all to attempt the impossible, as readers will already have understood. If we take the point of view of the questioner, Tozan's "three pounds of linen" is something absolutely inconceivable. Tozan points the way by thrusting his finger into the eye itself. Three pounds of linen was the same centuries ago as now. There is no difference in Buddhahood between the one who has realized it and the one who has yet to realize it. From the standpoint of the dharma body all beings are Buddhas. But Buddhas who instead of regarding themselves go round to others and ask about Buddha are no good, and Tozan's lion-roar of "three pounds of linen" cuts through with one stroke.

The self is Buddha, and there is not a fraction of distinction in their nature between any of the things of the world. Day and night the ever fresh spiritual activity goes on in the world, and in the little world of the self its Buddha acts all the time without eclipse. But living beings, especially human beings, have numerous cravings which obstruct the true spiritual activity. From one point of view, then, it is true that in so far as a man in his life resists cravings, he is showing progress and development.

The Buddha nature, as the truth in all, is certainly there from the beginning, but as regards its action we must know that spiritual practice is necessary. Shakyamuni, up to the time when he declared his attainment of Buddhahood, performed the great spiritual practices, and there has never been a Buddha or patriarch who did not do them. Just as the crude ore is refined in the furnace and then alone becomes real gold, and the jewel only when polished reveals its radiance, so we have to exert ourselves every day and night in the practices, that the Buddha nature may be

manifest. In the *Shobo Genzo* classic of Dogen it is explained:
"Every man is an instrument of the Buddha law. Never
once think yourself not so. By practice you will assuredly
have direct experience of it." Conversion means coming to
know that the self is Buddha; thereafter the path is the
advancing and relapsing of such an aspirant. It is not a
manifestation of some peculiar knowledge, or of a special
state; it is awakening to our fundamental nature. The path
must be followed faithfully. In the pilgrim and in the
woodcutter, the Buddha is acting. In bed or going about,
eating or washing, a Buddha is there too. To say "too" does
not mean that the Buddha is separate from self, a distinct
entity. The self is the Buddha. The Buddha work and
Buddha action is the working of the Buddha heart. The
Shobo Genzo says:

"When the Bodhisattva heart stirs, there is an impulse
to practise the way of the Buddhas. When this is being done
with partial devotion, it is found that in a hundred attempts
there is not one success. But in the end the passions come
under the sway of wisdom, or of the scriptural injunctions,
and then there can be success. And that success now *is* the
hundred failures of the past; it is the culmination of those
hundred failures."

When we turn the light and shine it within, we reverse
the current, and there is only the supreme Buddha heart,
only the Buddha's spiritual action, and the individual self
ceases to be. There are those who contemplate suicide in
the bitterness of failure in life. But for a Buddhist this is
pointless. When we fail, it is already progress to understand
that we have failed. We train ourselves by making that
failure a stepping-stone for a pace forward. The practice of
Buddhism is to realize that the present success is the hundred
failures of the past. When we understand that, no confusions
or disturbances will arise.

In Japan in ancient times there was a man called Kisukè
who looked after his aged parents with great devotion.

Often loose-living acquaintances used to tempt him with invitations to parties and wineshops, but he steadfastly refused. His reason was a very remarkable one. As a child he had received his physical body from his mother, and his mind (as it was thought) from his father. He used to decline the invitations by saying that he could not take his father and mother to the drinking parties. To the way of thinking of young people nowadays this may seem comical, but if we can get a hint from the story as to how to meet temptation we shall not fall into bad ways and later have nothing but regrets. Kisukè's sincerity, which would not conceal anything from his parents, is a manifestation in conduct of the pure Buddha heart. There are "modern" people who say that loyalty and devotion to parents are old-fashioned and not in the spirit of the times, but in regard to loyalty and devotion we do not have to think of new or old. They are the fundamental basis of human conduct. What a great mistake to listen to the erroneous spiritual teachings of the new sects which have sprung up after the war, and think that loyalty and love of parents can be lightly brushed aside! The spirit of tradition and the practice of compassion are manifested in this life, in accordance with the karma of past lives, as the relationship of parent and child. As it says in the poem by Sanetomo:

> Even birds and beasts which do not speak a word
> Have compassion, and the parent thinks of the child.

And true parents and children express loyalty and devotion to the full by their conduct, without talking about it.

At the beginning of the Tokugawa era there was a Zen priest named Suzuki Shosan, who at the end of his life came to live in the capital Edo (now Tokyo). Once several young *hatamoto* samurai came up and said to the old man: "The other day we were strolling and talking, and someone said that the gods and Buddhas do curse people. Some of us thought it was true, and some of us thought it was a lie. Everyone agreed we should try and see, so we turned our backs on the guardian god at the temple gate and made water there. Still nothing happened, so that the fact is the gods and Buddhas do not curse." As though he had not heard, Shosan was glaring fixedly in front of him, and then he shouted: "Brutes, brutes, brutes!" The bewildered samurai looked round stupidly, but could not see anything. Those accursed brutes who insulted the gods and Buddhas, the curse had been that they were reduced to bestial behaviour, that they became mere animals acting so. Thinking over his repeated shout of "Brutes!" we may also remember that a man who bows and prays to God or Buddha in order to get something for himself is only a vulgar beggar, and one who prays thinking himself great is a heretic. True virtue and the mind of faith are no more than the manifestation of the Buddha heart in conduct.

"This day let life be a noble life, even if it be a noble ruin. If we act in this spirit, body and mind will naturally be lovable, naturally honorable. Through our action the Buddha action becomes manifest, and we have attained the great way of the Buddhas." So the *Shushogi* classic explains to us on the basis of practical reality.

When we realize that our life today is the Buddha life, then we do not pass the day vainly. There will not arise the restlessness for pleasure and the constant disappointment. When a man no longer passes his days in vain, the Buddha action manifests and he can attain the Way. That day's action is the body of bliss. It is Buddha action alone and not what is called individual self. Where there is the egoity which says "I," the Buddha action does not appear. Those who perform bestial actions may be human in form but in conduct conform to animals. If we perform devilish actions, we have fallen to the state of demons. Those who follow the Buddha law and become without egoity, can perform the Buddha action. If we do the practice without relapsing, our daily life will bring the deep and direct experience of the grace of the Buddhas and patriarchs.

■ CHAPTER SIX

SINCE the war the state of the Japanese people has changed. Under the new Constitution, the attitude to the family, which before was the centre of Japanese life, has been altered, and the Emperor, previously regarded as supremely sacred, has become a symbol. It is easy to see that politically this democratization, by transferring to the people the sovereignty hitherto vested in the Emperor, has made the responsibilities of the people much greater. In brief it means that rights and duties must be properly observed, and the individual's position vis-à-vis his township or village, and also vis-à-vis the country, must be rightly understood and accepted. It is a mistake to think of democracy as a sort of present from America; it means an awakening of the people to themselves. In such an awakened community each exerts himself for the good of all. The Bodhisattva path, where the individual labours for others rather than for his own good, can be considered the basis of democratic government also. But since the war we see mainly a degeneration of morals, with people thinking that self-realization lies in satisfying their instinctive desires. The general attitude is to laugh at mention of the public good, and pursue selfish ends, indifferent to public abuses. As time passes, the wonderful human sympathy which was a part of Japan is reviving, but with things as they are now it is nonsense to speak of democracy. It is the rule of violence, the rule of barbarism. Morality arises from reflection on self. When we begin to realize that each day of life is worthy of honour, then a great and moral society can be formed. Democracy cannot develop properly among a people who simply act by instinct, unreflectingly, unashamed of unrighteousness and sin. To forget shame is to forget one's own true heart, the Buddha of truth in one's self. It comes from failing to respect one's own nature as a human being.

If there is self-awakening among individuals, morality will of itself spread to those above and those below, and democracy in the new Japan will be on a firm basis. If the people are not self-awakened, then however much the government is reformed and the Cabinet reshuffled, the state will never be right. The foundation of a really civilized state can only be developed from self-awakening of the individual through spiritual convictions.

To do everything for others and forget self is a special Buddhist doctrine. "Till all beings have been carried across to Nirvana, I will not become a Buddha. . . ." The main point of the Bodhisattva path in Mahayana is the vow that though in my whole life I do not become a Buddha, I will lift up all others to Buddhahood. Since the war, democracy has been proclaimed in Japan, but in fact this wonderful teaching has been known in Japan well over a thousand years. But when shame was forgotten, this spirit too was forgotten. It means to throw away self and work for others, and the real glory of it is when it is done without thinking consciously about it.

In the *Shobo Genzo* classic of Zen master Dogen it is said: "To attain the Buddha way means to attain self. To attain self means to forget self. To forget self means to realize the truth of everything. To realize that truth means to drop off body and mind from one's self and the self of others." He does not say "other people" but "the self of others." There is self in others also. It is not rejecting others and looking on their sufferings with indifference. The self forgets himself, losing himself in the self of others. Now one's self and the self of others vanish, and one attains wholly the world of truth. The trinkets of wealth or position or family disappear, but the real treasure of the Buddha heart begins to shine out. When in each that light shines out to meet the other lights, the rebuilding of Japan can take place in the light. To know of another's pain must be to take it as our own.

In the Kegon Sutra, it is related that the god Indra was on a mountain looking out. A goddess came and covered his eyes, but so strong was his power of vision that a third eye burst out between the brows. One day as he stood on the shore, he saw by the power of this third eye countless beautiful gems sparkling. In one was reflected the light of a second, and in that one again was reflected back the light of the first gem. The light of innumerable gems, reflected and again reflected back two, three, four times in each other — their beauty illumining each other is taken as a simile of the Net of Indra. And if in our democracy the hearts of the people open to reveal the Buddha light and in the same way illumine and reflect each other, then the country where such people live will be a model to the world.

With democracy came a tidal wave of "free thinking," but freedom never means acting selfishly and wilfully. Each has his own path, but that does not mean to act only selfishly. If we take the human body as an illustration, we cannot digest with the lungs or eat through the nose, but each has its own role, and following the prescribed course within those limits constitutes its freedom. "The bird flying as a bird, the fish going as a fish." When we get on a train, its direction and departure and arrival times are determined; our freedom is in making use of it. It is the same in our whole life. We cannot disturb the order which is at the very heart of freedom.

Again, when they speak of equal rights, it must not be an envious levelling down. The Emperor is called a citizen, but he differs from us in that he is a symbol of the state. In that capacity he has no obligation to pay taxes, but on the other hand he is not free to marry just anyone, nor can he enter commerce. He would not be permitted to open a department store if he wanted to. Then, for instance, when we pray for the perpetuation of the Imperial line, it is clear that his position is quite distinct from that of us ordinary people.

From the Buddhist point of view, real greatness is in releasing the Buddha light. As one reaches this grand state he sees it in others also, and when others bow in worship, he himself bows to them. Harmony lies in taking a step back into humility and self-effacement. When the Buddha heart prompts this step back, the light of peace becomes manifest, and a democracy filled with love comes into being.

We should resolve to build the state rightly out of virtuous lives based on spiritual realization of the selfless Buddha heart, namely the Buddha heart of Zen, and so realize the happiness and fortune for which men long. Weapons may stave off for a time the dreaded Red ideology, but to entrust ourselves to a democracy which merely cloaks the arrogance of some political "boss" would equally be the end of all hope of peace and prosperity.

■ CHAPTER SEVEN

AS ZEN has a totally unrestricted and universal outlook, among the "cases" or koan, reputedly seventeen hundred in number, there are stories about kittens and dogs, about turtles, and about water buffaloes. The fifty-sixth case of the Chinese anthology of Abbot Wanshi, the *Shoyoroku*, is the story called "The White Hare of Master Misshi." In such stories everything in the world—sun, moon, and stars, the voice of the valley stream and the colours of the mountain, the wind in the pines and the rain on the bamboos— is pressed into service to teach. The great truth of Zen manifests itself, filling the earth and filling the heaven. The ancients could pick up anything at all and say: "This is It." They made their Zen koan out of anything that came to hand. The inmost spirit of Zen is that everything is treasure in our own home.

Among the Zen cases, then, is the story of the White Hare of Misshi. One day a white hare ran across in front of him, and he and his fellow master Tozan used it as the occasion for their Zen. This is the Case of the White Hare. But as in the fable of the hare and the tortoise, the real point is not contained in the literal interpretation. Still, it is important to appreciate how skilfully in the dialogue the two masters manipulate the theme of the hare. First let us look at the case as it appears in the anthology.

The case: Misshi and Tozan were walking together when they saw a white hare run across in front of them. Misshi remarked: "How quick!"

Tozan said: "How so?"

Misshi: "Like a white-robed (commoner) achieving the dignity of premier."

Tozan: "Oh venerable, oh great!" and other phrases.

Misshi: "How so yourself!"

Tozan: "The cords which have tied on the nobleman's hat for generations suddenly fall away."

The words "the case" at the beginning mean the formal presentation of a Zen koan, namely that there is now being given an incident between the ancient masters from the old records. Tozan was the founder of our Soto sect in China; Misshi, like Tozan, was a disciple of the master Ungan, so that they were fellow students under the same master.

They were once walking together along a mountain path when a white hare darted across in front of them. Misshi remarked how quickly it had gone. Tozan asked: "How so?" He puts a penetrating question, and with this thrust by Tozan the story of the white hare is no longer an ordinary incident but becomes a koan. Now in the discussion universal truth is contained in the one white hare.

Misshi at once replied: "Like a white-robed achieving the dignity of premier." In China the "white-clad" meant the common people, and there could be no quicker success in the world than for one of the commoners to become premier at one jump. He expresses the Zen principle of not dabbling in the labyrinth of logic and academic discussion, but entering at one stroke: the passions are realization, birth-and-death is Nirvana, living beings are the truth-body of the Buddha. This unwavering upward-looking consciousness is the mark of a genius who kicks down every obstacle. Misshi, looking ever upward, takes the white hare above the clouds. But against this, Tozan has the freedom to look down and shows the way to set the white hare free in the fields. He pretends to express great veneration and admiration, but that expression contains a reproof that Misshi is yet unripe. Misshi cannot understand and retorts: "How so yourself!" Tozan replies that the cords which have held the noble's hat for generations quickly fall away. His meaning is that a man, though born into a noble family which for generations has worn the ceremonial hat, can fall in one hour. He falls—but he is a Buddha child, and so far as he is conscious of that, he may when needful take a fall without loss of poise.

From the absolute point of view, universal truth is certainly something noble, profound, and eternal. But following the law of association (karma), the moon in the sky lodges its reflection in the puddle left by the horse's tread. So the subtle body of the Truth, according to association, becomes an earthworm, becomes a frog, a badger, a hare. With the "falling away of the cords," it is not only things accounted high which are Truth. If it were only the great ones, there would be many difficulties. Tozan's view is that the hare is just right as it is, and we should not merely look at the strength of its legs for jumping but savour a taste of Zen when it appears just as it is before the eyes. The white hare which for Misshi was to be cloud-hidden, lifted above the skies, is once more released in the meadow and given its freedom.

Some one will ask: "Well, which side is the victor?" Both of them are skilled marshals of words, and each of the views, one upward-looking and the other downward, is doctrinally quite sound. Still, from the Zen standpoint, the view of Misshi, which attains the heights and remains there exclusively, flying in the heavens, must be taken as surpassed by the downward-turning view of Tozan, which gives freedom in the mountains and fields. On a high place there is generally the danger of a fall, and this means a loss of freedom; but the one who is already down has no fear of falling and moves about in freedom. And particularly in the case of a hare!

So in Zen we are always told to take one step more from the top of the hundred-foot bamboo, to leave the danger of the high places and go on the path of safety. That path means just ordinariness. It is ordinariness, but different from the former ordinariness. It is like the case of cold water. Cold water which has not been boiled must be different from cold water which has been through boiling. So with ordinariness: that before satori is very different from the ordinariness of after satori.

What is this ordinariness? It is things being what they properly are. Men being men, and women women, the business man being a business man and the scholar a scholar. As it says in the *Zazen-gi*: "The bird flying as a bird, the fish going as a fish." In this everyday life there is nothing strange or marvellous, and this is the basis of Zen. Official *as* an official, merchant as merchant, farmer as farmer, student as student, husband as husband and wife as wife— if they act *as* the part implies they can have peace and be at rest. They will have no disturbing thoughts and will not be passing meaninglessly through the light and shade of time. Each day of their ordinary life will be noble.

In the true doctrine there are no miracles, but it is this sort of everyday human life. There is nothing extraordinary in it. The great master says: "Everyday mind is the way." To be able to return and settle in normality is the final stage of Zen. Put like this, it seems nothing. But this forgetting of aspirations and returning, as it were a fish or a bird, is the life of greatness, and if we look at the difficulties we see it is hard indeed. Bansho too says it is easy to mount from earth to heaven, but hard to descend from there. In Zen it is easy to trumpet the upward looking view, but then very hard to return to the despised everyday life. They know the way out and forget the way back. But without this returning home and sitting at rest, Zen is only a ghost.

To sum up the Zen process: just as the sweating war-horses are lashed and the thousand swords mobilized only that the land may return to peace and each to his calling, so the real demonstration of Zen is to show the essential element of serenity in life. Tozan raises his banner on behalf of this return to peace. Still, it is only when that state of Misshi has been passed through that this is born, and it is by passing through both these views that one can experience the real taste of Zen. Zen master Wanshi says in one of his verses on the koan called "The Kindness of Jizo":

"Travelling till sick of travelling, now it is as it was; the veils disentangled, I have reached not-knowing. Let it be short or let it be long, have done with cutting off and tacking on. Following where it is high and following where it is low, things even out of themselves. As the circumstances are rich or straitened, act accordingly; walk supremely at leisure in the fields as your feet take you."

If we can make our gait in life supremely at leisure, then the great master Tozan will admit us unreservedly to his friendship and company.

■ CHAPTER EIGHT

ONE OBJECT of Zen is of course to see one's nature and be enlightened, but that is not the final resting-place. Zen embraces Buddhism and it is the practice of the Buddha way. What is Buddhism then, and what is the Buddha way? Many people have an idea that Buddhism is just tales about heaven and hell, and how to lay out the body for a funeral, or maybe some little old man talking about resignation. So young people especially tend to turn away as from something that has not any value for them. They do not understand what real Buddhism is. It is the truth of the universe; it is grasping the absolute; it is the great enlightenment of Shakyamuni Buddha. That truth is universal—so fine it can be contained on the tip of a cormorant's feather, so vast that it transcends space into infinity. Truth absolute is the life of Buddhism, and the question is how to grasp it.

The Diamond Sutra teaches: "What is called Buddhism is no Buddhism." What Shakyamuni taught for forty-nine years as his doctrine was only explanation to help people come to direct knowledge. The real life of Buddhism is not there. As he said: "Know that my teachings are metaphors, as it were a raft." A raft or boat is only used until the objective, the far shore, is reached.

Where is the real Buddhism which is the objective? When it has been sought and reached, we come to rest in the everyday, in the ordinary, without anything abnormal about it. The ordinary man suffers because he cannot be at rest in ordinariness. "I went, but after all it was nothing special"—human life is full of such disappointments, things not turning out as expected. From the viewpoint of enlightenment, truth is the normal. It is not something special. The willow is green, the flower red, the fire hot, and the wind ever moving. Zen master Dogen in the *Zazen-shin* gives the conclusion of Zen: "The bird flying as a bird, the fish going as a fish." So it means the normal state of things. If we think of Buddhism as just a wonderful philosophy, it is because we do not see that it is normality, ordinariness, the daily life of eating and drinking. The truth is not outside daily life.

In Zen, while a man feels unable to approach the upward-looking koan which is given him by the teacher, he fights with the tongue-sword and brandishes the spear. But when he reaches the perfectly unfettered Zen-in-action, he sees into the koan which appears of itself naturally before him, and then the real life begins.

A monk asked Joshu: "What is this Buddhism?" Immediately he replied: "The tree in the courtyard." There happened to be a tree in the court in front of the master's room, and without a hair of hesitation he made use of it. This is living Buddhism.

Again, a monk asked Abbot Seigen: "What is the great principle of Buddhism?" Having heard that this monk had just come from a place called Roryo, the abbot answered: "What is the price of rice in the Roryo market?" In his Zen-in-action the rice-market is taken to show the great principle of Buddhism.

A lay disciple who was a follower of Zen master Yakusan asked: "What is the truth?" Yakusan pointed up and down. "Have you got it?" But the disciple could not understand: "No." Then Yakusan added: "Cloud in the blue sky, water in the jar." The disciple was suddenly enlightened. The truth is just this cloud in the blue sky, water in the jar; not some abnormal phenomenon but the natural splendour of the mountains, rivers, and plains. Truly this is a level and simple Way.

There is one more of these tales from China, an interesting one about Joshu, to whom a monk came for the first time and said: "I have just entered the monastery. Please give me some instruction." In a monastery the monks take rice-gruel in the morning and evening for their meal. Joshu asked: "Have you had your rice-gruel?" He meant: have you had the morning meal? The monk answered directly: "Yes, I have had it," and Joshu said: "Then wash your bowl." All this has a meaning, and it is one of the koan. Bansho says about it: "When it is meal-time, open your mouth; when it is bed-time, shut your eyes; when you wash your face, clean the nostrils; when you put on sandals, fit them on to the feet." When washing the face, we become aware if our nose is dirty; when putting on sandals, we have to slip them properly over our toes.

The final resting-place of Zen, the life of Buddhism, is Zen-in-action, not going astray from the natural activity in ordinary everyday life. So, even unknowingly, day and night we are in the Buddha law and applying it. Then what need for enlightenment and training? "Going is Zen, sitting too is Zen." But no. Water that has been first boiled and then allowed to cool is certainly different from ordinary water, though both are equally cool. There must be a difference too between the ordinary man and the disciple who has undergone a long training. If there were not, admittedly Zen realization would be useless. They are alike as equally within the Buddha law, but the point of difference is that one follows the way with delight and the other does not. Though swimming in the same water, the man who has his clothes on is hampered because his body does not move freely through the water. Again, just as two people facing but separated by a pane of glass cannot talk to each other, so we are immersed in the holy truth but as it were cut off by glass. Somehow the glass has to be got away; somehow the swimmer has to discard the clothes—this is the absolute necessity for seeing the nature and being enlightened. To put it more concretely: the unenlightened has not realized his self. Because he lacks self-realization, his ideas are at the mercy of every fluctuating fashion, and he is swayed by every rumour. His object in life never goes a step beyond pleasure, wealth, fame, and profit. But the disciple who earnestly seeks truth steps outside that routine and realizes the self; then the immortal truth arises in what is mortal. This is the real life, when practice and realization are one. Finally he reaches the ultimate goal of Zen, to adapt freely to the world. Now the parents are like parents, the children like children, the husband like a husband, and the wife like a wife. The willow is green and the flower red, the bird flying as a bird and the fish going as a fish.

When each is at peace in his own part, he can contribute to the real glory of the nation and then there is the power to create a lasting culture. We call it ordinary life, and it is, but this is also the Truth unchanged throughout the ages. See! When it is cold the bird perches on the tree, the duck takes to the water. Each repairs only to its own refuge. The truth is the truth in each. Neither is better—there is no better or worse because there is no inequality. Where there is no inequality, the heart is tranquil and the world radiates the light of peace. This is our Soto Zen, and it is the final resting-place of Zen.

Hakuin's "Song of Meditation"

A COMMENTARY BY

AMAKUKI SESSAN

ABBOT AMAKUKI delivered these lectures over the Kyoto Radio early in the 1930's, and soon afterwards revised them for publication. There are certain peculiarities of style for which the reader should be prepared. To illustrate the Zen principle that sacred and everyday are not distinct, he sets the sonorous Chinese monosyllables of the sutras against light Japanese colloquialisms; compassion and irony, sublimity and familiarity, are deliberately juxtaposed.

He has a special technique of repetition of a key phrase in different contexts; this is a hint for working on the koan. Another well-known feature of Zen style is to punctuate a narrative with short comments, sometimes no more than ejaculations, to point the incidents of the story.

Readers will notice the fondness for a concrete illustration rather than a universal principle, and for action rather than abstraction; these are characteristic of Japanese Zen, particularly in its expression as poetry.

THE SONG OF MEDITATION

All beings are from the very beginning Buddhas.
It is like water and ice:
Apart from water, no ice,
Outside living beings, no Buddhas.
Not knowing it is near, they seek it afar. What a pity!
It is like one in the water who cries out for thirst;
It is like the child of a rich house who has strayed away among the
  poor.
The cause of our circling through the six worlds
Is that we are on the dark paths of ignorance.
Dark path upon dark path treading,
When shall we escape from birth-and-death?
The Zen meditation of the Mahayana
Is beyond all our praise.
Giving and morality and the other perfections,
Taking of the Name, repentance, discipline,
And the many other right actions,
All come back to the practice of meditation.
By the merit of a single sitting
He destroys innumerable accumulated sins.
How should there be wrong paths for him?
The Pure Land paradise is not far.
When in reverence this truth is heard even once,
He who praises it and gladly embraces it has merit without end.
How much more he who turns within
And confirms directly his own nature,
That his own nature is no-nature—
Such has transcended vain words.
The gate opens, and cause and effect are one;

Straight runs the way—not two, not three.
Taking as form the form of no-form,
Going or returning, he is ever at home.
Taking as thought the thought of no-thought,
Singing and dancing, all is the voice of truth.
Wide is the heaven of boundless Samadhi,
Radiant the full moon of the fourfold wisdom.
What remains to be sought? Nirvana is clear before him,
This very place the Lotus paradise, this very body the Buddha

■ CHAPTER ONE

All beings are from the very beginning Buddhas.
It is like water and ice:
Apart from water, no ice,
Outside living beings, no Buddhas.

THE SONG OF MEDITATION

IN THE original the *Song of Meditation* is in very easy
language. Before Hakuin (1685–1768), Zen in Japan had
not quite given up its Chinese flavour, but with him it
became completely Japanese. Previously too it had a somewhat aristocratic outlook, but he popularized it and made it
universal. If Muso Kokushi (1275–1351) of Tenryuji temple, the teacher of emperors, represents aristocratic Zen, we
may see Hakuin as the representative of the people's Zen.
His Zen is austere and yet universal, like towering Mount
Fuji, to which everyone can look up from wherever he is.
Hakuin's Zen is an eternal luminary in the spiritual firma-
ment and a supreme contribution to Japanese culture.

4 (opposite). ZEN MASTER HAKUIN.
This self-portrait, painted in 1768, shortly before Hakuin's death
at eighty-three, shows the master in ceremonial robes and carrying
a *hossu*.

Though the Song is so easy to follow, yet it contains Hakuin's profoundest and most mystical doctrine. Of course, as to attaining his First Principle, which speech and thought cannot reach, each man has to realize that for himself. If words or thought could grasp it, then it would be already only a second or third principle. In these lectures the Song will be explained as far as possible in a simple and popular way which can be understood by anyone who cares to read.

"All beings are from the very beginning Buddhas." "All beings" is the classical Buddhist phrase, but we can take it as referring principally to us human beings. This one phrase, "all beings are from the very beginning Buddhas," is the centre and beginning and end of the whole Song. We in this world of illusion, and the Buddhas in the world of realization are from the very beginning one and not two. Illusion and realization are not two! The oneness of Buddhas and all beings is here proclaimed outright. If we can grasp this phrase completely, the rest of the Song will be easy. It is the centre and beginning and end not only of the Song of Meditation, but the forty-nine years' preaching of Shakyamuni Buddha was in essence the same truth, and the 84,000 gates of the Law are none other than this.

All beings are from the very beginning Buddhas. Buddha means an awakened man, an enlightened man. The word carries the meaning of deliverance from all bonds and fetters and ties. He awakes himself, then awakens others; that is to say, he is perfect both in realization and in spiritual action. He has realization, action, and perfection. The Buddha has three bodies: first the body of truth such as Vairochana Buddha, the Buddha of Truth, whose form is all-pervading. His tongue the stream in the valley, his pure body the colours of the mountain—the wind and the light, the hills, rivers, grass, and trees, all are this truth-body of the Buddha. The second is the body of bliss; by virtue of his holy practices the ideal Buddha like Amitabha appears in an ideal form. The third is the body of physical manifestation, which is the Buddha who appears as a man, the so-called historical Buddha, a Buddha like Shakyamuni, who appeared in India. These three bodies, the truth-body, bliss-body, and manifesting body, express the three aspects of the Buddha—essence, form, and action.

But this Buddha and ourselves are not separate. All beings are from the very beginning Buddhas. It is the same truth as in the famous phrases that the passions are the bodhi, that Sansara or birth-and-death is Nirvana. Being in the world of illusion is called "living being," and being in the world of realization is called "Buddha." When deluded, a living being; when enlightened, a Buddha. The Buddhas are the living beings, ignorance is enlightenment, enlightenment is ignorance, the Buddhas and living beings are the same. It is related in the Avatansaka Sutra that after six years of intense practice, on the eighth day of the twelfth month under the bodhi tree, Shakyamuni saw the morning star and suddenly had the great realization (satori). His first utterance was: "Wonder, wonder! All living beings are endowed with the Buddha wisdom and virtue!" Another account says it was in these words: "When a Buddha attains and sees the truth-world, grasses, trees, earth—all, all become Buddhas!" In other words the Buddha nature is ever perfect in each and every one of us. The Prajnaparamita Hridaya Sutra says that form is the void and the void is form. The relationship between the Buddhas and living beings is exactly like that. The Sutra does not say that the world of forms, the material things, is annihilated and then the void is attained, or that out of the void, as reality, the world of forms is manifested. The world of forms as it is now is the void, and similarly the void without changing manifests the form-world of mountains, rivers, and earth. (See Plate 5.)

The successive Buddhas and lines of patriarchs have taught in various ways the oneness of Buddhas and living beings and have given different illustrations, but Hakuin thunders directly at us: "All living beings are from the very beginning Buddhas!" This is the characteristic living method of his Zen. There is no holding back; it is a true lion roar. We are always thinking of getting away from this shore of illusion and attaining some farther shore of realization, of getting out of the state of the ordinary man and reaching the world of the Buddhas; we take illusion and satori (realization) as opposites and the ordinary man and the Buddha as quite separate, different as fire and water. We wander desperately about where the road forks, one path "to illusion" and the other "to satori." Now Hakuin fearlessly shouts that all living beings are from the very beginning Buddhas. His great cry proclaims tersely and clearly the sense of the passage in the Sutra of Perfect Wisdom: "When we come to know that all living beings are from the very beginning Buddhas, then Sansara and Nirvana both are like last night's dream." Nothing stands between living beings and Buddhas, between illusion and realization. The point is skilfully made in Hakuin's next phrase, "It is like water and ice: apart from water no ice, outside living beings no Buddhas." To show the absolute oneness of ordinary men and Buddhas, he adduces ice, which is fundamentally water. Apart from water there can be no ice; that very piece of ice is just the water, and the water is just the ice. When frozen it is ice; when melted it is water. If you search in the water, you will not find any ice. But the ice comes from the water. Daito Kokushi has a verse on this:

Search in the water and you will not find the waves,
Yet the waves arise from the water.

Abbot Sengai's comment is interesting:

The Buddha is the deliverer, just because of the sorrows of the world.

If there are no more sorrows, then from what is he deliverer?

The word "ice" is significant. Water, when exposed to

cold, freezes, hardens, and becomes ice, and though its nature does not change, it loses complete freedom of movement. So through illusion of ignorance, the human being sets and hardens, and though his Buddha-nature does not change, he is debarred from the limitless freedom of the Buddha. But just as the ice, set and hardened by the cold, is still in fact all water, so the human being, set and hardened by illusion, is still in fact all Buddha.

There is a difficulty. If we say ice and water are the same thing, after all they aren't, are they? If we went to buy ice we should not accept water. It is not a relation of identity. Yet we cannot say that they are not the same thing, because apart from water there is no ice. So it is not a relation of difference either. Ice and water are not identical and not different. The relation between Buddha and ourselves is just like that. If it is said we are the same thing—well, we are not. We are not the same thing. But if it is said we are separate, we are not. We are not different. So we are neither the same nor different. To apply heat and melt ice is a round-about way of knowing it is water, but when we realize that the ice just as it stands is water, we can appreciate the water in the ice. Living beings as they stand are Buddhas, and when we realize it we can appreciate the Buddha-essence in the living beings.

Since the ice is frozen hard, it cannot adapt itself to the shape of a vessel as water can. The human being, set and hardened by illusion, has not the spiritual power to act in unlimited freedom. When the ice is melted, the water regains its freedom, and so by dissolving the illusion we can acquire freedom and use it spiritually. The difference is just whether the ice is melted or not. When the human body is rigid, it is of little use. It is not healthy. In Zen it is a question of rigidity not of body but of mind. The difference between Buddha and ordinary man is not form, but whether or not there is the rigidity of mind. (With ice and water the difference is not of content but of outer form, and the analogy cannot be pushed too far.) If by one revolution of the mind we can get rid of its rigidity, then we are perfect Buddhas as we stand. It is the rigidity of mind which is the cause of all the trouble.

In the *Awakening of Faith* classic there is the famous simile in which the Absolute and Sansara are likened to water and waves, but Hakuin skilfully substitutes water and ice and, by introducing the characteristic rigidity of ice, deepens the meaning. Seeing this one as an ignorant man and that one as a Buddha is the illusion, and it means being still in the state of making distinctions; when freed from this state there is no ignorant man and no Buddha, but the body as it stands is Buddha. This is the state of freedom and non-distinction. People are vainly seeking the Buddha in distant places, and want a paradise on the far shore. Each from his special viewpoint makes distinctions between this one and that, not realizing that all are from the very beginning Buddhas. In pity for our vain pursuit of shadows Hakuin is telling us: "Not knowing it is near, they seek it afar. What a pity!"

The truth is not the special preserve of Hakuin. The Lotus Sutra says clearly: "O disciple, the Buddha's wisdom and virtue are present everywhere. And why? Because there is no living being which is not endowed with them. But clinging to confused and contrary notions, they do not realize it. When they leave their wrong thinking, universal natural and infinite wisdom will manifest in them. The Buddha, perfect in the fourfold wisdom, pities us that we do not know the Buddha within us." In the Nirvana Sutra it is written, "All, all have the Buddha nature, but it cannot be seen when covered by the passions." In the Sutra of the Sixth Patriarch: "The worldly man from the beginning is naturally endowed with the wisdom of prajna, but because he is deluded he cannot realize it for himself." The Buddha seed is everywhere, the Buddha nature is possessed by all, just as wherever you dig the earth you will come to water.

色即是空
空即是色

日本曹洞禅宗
管長高階瓏仙

5. CALLIGRAPHY BY TAKASHINA ROSEN.
"Form itself is the Void; the Void itself is form." (See page 71.)
This is in the stiff style of calligraphy known as *kaisho*. Compare
Plates 8 and 12, in which the poems are in the "grass" or fluent
style.

Only plant them, and anywhere flowers will grow;
It is the mind that makes the meanness of the body.

Digging or not digging, planting or not planting, that is the point.

We must get rid of delusions and leave our attachment, to see things anew from an awakened standpoint. The Buddha is awake, and an awakened man is enlightened. He has not really acquired anything new, but has woken from the illusion and veiling of ignorance. It is putting off the coloured spectacles. While wearing the coloured glasses of egoity and partiality, whatever colour we see, red or blue, it is never the true colour. While bound in the dream of confused and contrary thinking, existence and non-existence both are no more than figments of a dream.

An ancient says of this: "While in the state of illusion, the four affirmations are each wrong; in the state of realization each of them is correct," and he gives the illustration of a fragrant blossom on a tree in the garden. In the state of illusion we see it and say that it exists. And yet, it does not, for before it appeared on the branch, and again three days from now, where is it? But it would be wrong to say it does not exist—is it not a fact, with its sweet smell, right before us? Though it may fall, yet the fruit will appear, and then next year will it not come again, tempted into bloom by the spring breeze? Again it would be wrong to say that it neither is nor is not, and wrong also to say that it both is and is not. It is, it is not, it neither is nor is not, it both is and is not—all the four affirmations are wrong. But once looked at from the standpoint of satori, it is right to explain that it is, right to teach that it is not, right again that it neither is nor is not, and there is no bar to saying it both is and is not. All four statements are right. When there is real mother love, it is right when she pets the child, and right again when she scolds it, and right when she neither pets nor scolds, and right again sometimes to pet and sometimes to scold. But suppose it is a spiteful stepmother who secretly hates the little one; then, petting or scolding, it is always wrong. In other words, speaking of existence or non-existence correctly or not depends entirely on having re-alization.

We must awaken from this present dream state and become able to see things rightly. Abbot Muju warns us how deep is the illusion:

> In the long night's sleep, another sleep;
> Within the dream, seeing yet another dream.

An old verse says:

> In this dream world, when he tells to another what he has dreamt,
> The telling of the dream too is only a dream.

People think they have broken the dream, but it was only the dream within the dream, and they are still dreaming, sunk in darkness, writhing about, their whole life a sleep and the end a dream-dying. How pitiable was Chitosè when he went to Abbot Daitetsu, wearing the face of satori, calling it all a dream but still sunk in that dream! And the abbot replied:

> "So it is all a dream, nothing at all? . . .
> Why what a vulgar fool you are!"

When we are awakened by the lion-roar: "All beings are from the very beginning Buddhas," we can see that illusion and realization are not two, that purity and defilement also are not two. We can see everything as it really is. We can accept the world as no different from Buddhahood. In the sutra it is said: "When sticking attachment arises in Buddhahood, that is the world; when in the world sticking attachment is left off, that is Buddhahood." The Kegon Sutra explains: "Buddhahood is not opposed to the world, nor the world opposed to Buddhahood." When sticking attachment is left off, we can see the forms of things as they are, and in the truth of things there is no purity or impurity, as the Prajnaparamita Hridaya Sutra says. When blossoms are on the bough they are pure; when they fall they become litter. Saliva in the mouth is pure, but when it falls it becomes spittle. Hair is clean on the head but gives offence if it falls on food. We speak according to our feeling of things as pure or impure, but in themselves the things are neither pure nor impure. Adults do not like to drink from the same cup in succession. They won't do it. Children will pass round a cake, biting it one after another, but try to get them to do it when they have grown up! This is because there is a sticking attachment to selfhood.

That all beings are from the very beginning Buddhas is the roar of Hakuin himself, but the teaching is the very life of Mahayana Buddhism and appears everywhere. The first step, nay the very basis, of the religious life is to have faith that all living beings are from the beginning Buddhas. Instead of regarding ourselves as descendants of monkeys or as servants of God (though in one sense it may be true), the great thing is to spur ourselves on by deepening our awakening to self, faith in self, respect for self. The Nirvana Sutra teaches: "All, all have the Buddha nature, but it cannot be seen when covered by the passions." The main thing in realizing Buddhahood and obtaining liberation is to leave our passionate attachments. More properly, it is to penetrate to the source of the mind whence the waves of passionate attachment arise. In the *Shodoka* poem, Yoka Daishi says that the present illusory nature is in fact the Buddha nature, and this empty body with its phenomenal transformations is in fact the truth-body of the Buddha. We must recognize this as a fact and then realize it in experience. The Third Patriarch in his *Shinjimmei* classic has the phrase: "The Way is not difficult; it just means distaste for picking and choosing." Further there is the phrase: "just be without love and hate, and all is clear as running water." In brief, the essence of the process is this: just once throw away everything. Love and hate, picking and choosing, throw them all away —the no-difficulty-of-the-Way as well—and have done with the clear running water. He who thus renounces all and renounces the attachment to all, can truly possess all.

Renunciation and giving up must not be misunderstood as mere negation. Look at our men of possessions these days, the possessors of rank, of fame, yes and even of scholarship. What do they do? The scholar is trapped by scholarship, the man of rank and fame by rank and fame, and the rich man by his wealth. They are afflicted by it; they have to labour for it; and instead of being able to use it they are burdened by it. Because of their sticking attachment they can never throw it away. They are no more than keepers for it. To leave all, to throw away all, is the real way to pick up all and possess all. For such a man, possessions, whatever they may be, are not an obstacle. He can use them, and they become sources of glory and virtue.

> *When I think of it as part of me*
> *It is light—the snow on my straw hat!*

It is not a burden. And so with the moon, the flowers, the towering cliffs—this is the world of the great line: "In that not-a-single-thing is endless treasure!" *(Plate 6)* Mahayana and especially Zen realization puts the label *equal* on living beings and Buddhas, who by ordinary standards are totally different in every way.

Obviously when there is delusion or attachment or blind hankering in our mind, we cannot see through to the real nature of things, and it is extreme foolishness that we leave our Buddhahood and suffer the agonies of lost children. We all know what it is to suffer in the stifling heat of a tropical summer. Hakuin wrote a poem on a picture of the cool of the evening:

> *The sleeve which is carrying nothing is light—*
> *The evening cool!*

and on a picture of Bodhidharma on the reed leaves at evening:

> *Resting on the leaves of good and bad—*
> *The evening cool!*

The empty sleeves are light; good and bad are trodden

underfoot; crossing beyond, we find this coolness of spirit, free from hankerings and attachment—the Buddha always in the self. There is a famous poem by Saint Honen:

The clouds cleared and now has come the light—
Do not think like this.
From the beginning in the sky
Was always the radiant dawn moon.

Never have living beings and Buddhas been strangers. Apart from Buddhas, no living beings; outside living beings, no Buddhas. We must realize this most intimate relation, nay identity. The old verse runs:

What is the Buddha?
The moss carpet around the rock
Displays that very form.

In the Heikè epic is a song:

The Buddha in the beginning is an ordinary man;
We in the end are Buddhas.
Endowed every one with the Buddha-nature,
How tragic to be separated from it!

Living beings and Buddhas are no strangers, and furthermore without the one there is not the other. The example is given of ice and water: as apart from water no ice, so outside living beings no Buddhas. We should meditate deeply on these words, bringing our mind to stillness, to taste the real meaning. In fact, better than putting legs onto the snake (which does not need them) with these foolish comments of mine, is to light an incense stick before the Buddha image and reverently meditate on the Song of Meditation.

What has been said in this chapter? It is this: that living beings are from the very beginning Buddhas. The wooden Buddha is burnt in the fire, the clay Buddha dissolved in the water, the metal Buddha melted in the furnace. Somehow we have to grasp the true Buddha.

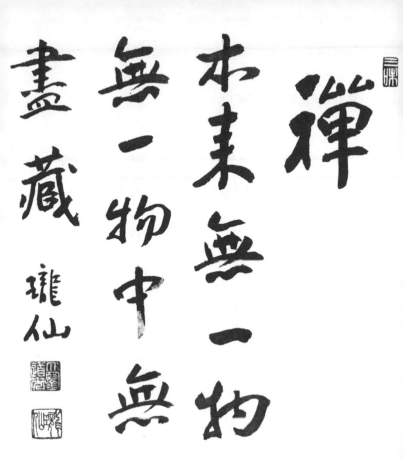

6. CALLIGRAPHY BY TAKASHINA ROSEN: ZEN.
"From the very beginning, not a single thing. In that not-a-single-thing is inexhaustible treasure." (See page 79.) The style of calligraphy is nearer the running hand, midway between stiff and "grass." Notice the beautifully firm strokes. The *raku-hitsu* is the top left stroke of the character 禅 (Zen). (See pages 226–27.)

CHAPTER TWO

Not knowing it is near, they seek it afar. What a pity!
It is like one in the water who cries out for thirst;
It is like the child of a rich house who has strayed away
among the poor.

THE SONG OF MEDITATION

THESE three lines explain further the great declaration that all living beings are from the very beginning Buddhas. The relation between Buddha and ordinary man is so close, so intimate, that it is not noticed, as the eyebrow, being so close to the eye, is not visible. The sage Confucius has remarked how pitiable are those who seek afar the Way which is near. The Christian Bible too has "Repent ye, for the Kingdom of Heaven is at hand" and similar phrases. The Amitayur Dhyana Sutra, describing paradise, says clearly it is no long journey.

A man came to see Muso Kokushi, the Zen master who founded Tenryuji temple in Saga Prefecture in Japan, and asked: "What is it that they call the wonderful law?" In other words, what is the Buddha law? Now Muso Kokushi replied: "The fish is in the water but does not know the water; man is in the wonderful law but does not know the law." The fish is born in water, grows up in water, lives in water, but because he is so close to the water he does not know it. There is a subtle point here. If the fish goes out of the water to look at it so that he can say: "Aha! so *that* is water!" then he dies. Can the anatomist find the life principle by cutting up a healthy person's body? On the contrary, he kills the life. We are born of the wonderful law, nourished by it and living by it, from beginning to end never apart from it. But we are so close that we do not perceive it. In Zen they speak of the relation between the Buddha law and ourselves, between the Buddhas and living beings, in such phrases as "the mind, the Buddha" and "this very body the Buddha." Again it is taught to shine our light right down where we stand and not be sidetracked.

The disciples are all the time radiant with spiritual light, Zen master Rinzai tells them solemnly, and apart from the listeners to his sermon where should there be Buddhas? When this profound doctrine is understood, all sidetracking is ended. A monkey, seeing the moon's reflection in the water, rushes to seize it. Hakuin warns us in the Song against such persistent folly, warns us not to be like the man in the middle of the water crying with thirst, not to stray like the rich man's child among the poor. Imagine a man up to his neck in water but croaking with thirst; imagine the rich man's heir who has wandered away and is now a beggar, haunting the back streets and holding out his sleeve for alms. This last illustration is taken from the famous story in the Lotus Sutra, where the nobleman's son wanders away as a child and becomes a homeless vagrant. In time he forgets that he ever had a home, but one day without thinking he comes to the gate of the lord's house. He has no faintest notion that he was born there, but stands at the gate imploring pity for his wretchedness. The noble sees him from within and recognizes his long-lost son even after all those years, but when he calls him to come in, the miserable beggar is frightened and will not. So he first arranges that he be taken in as the humblest servant, and then little by little promoted, until finally he again resumes his name, when the house and its wealth and treasure all become his.

Living beings are from the very beginning Buddhas; we have from the beginning the Buddha nature but have forgotten it, have left our home and become entangled in contrary and confused thinking, so ending as wanderers on the six paths and dwellers in the three worlds of suffering. As the child of a rich house strays away among the poor— aren't the agonies and sufferings of the people nowadays just like that? Why do they not return to their spiritual nature and find out the root of their sufferings? Seeking a Buddha outside, rushing to get away from this world and find some ideal world somewhere else—it is like being in the water but forgetting the fact and moving about looking for water. Being in the Buddha, surrounded by the Buddha, yet raising our voice and calling out for the Buddha!

Long ago in China, Ekai entered upon the Zen training under the great Baso. The master asked: "Where have you come from?"

"From the Great Cloud Temple in Etsu."

"What do you want here?"

"I came to seek Buddhism. I am here to ask you to tell me your Buddhism."

"I have none. What Buddhism should you seek?"

The master told him that he would get nothing by over-looking the treasure at home and seeking from others.

Ekai asked: "What is this treasure which Ekai has?"

The master said: "That which now asks me, that is the treasure. It has all, and lacks nothing at all. You have it at hand. How is it that you are seeking it from others?"

This plunged Ekai into reflection. In the light of this story we can go deeper into Hakuin's man in the water parched with thirst and the rich man's son straying among the poor.

In ancient India holy Vasubandhu was honoured by all for his strict observance of discipline, long hours of prayer, purity, and renunciation. To remove this one-sided view, the patriarch Gayata asked one of the disciples of Vasu-bandhu: "Will he reach Buddhahood by these austerities and earnest discipline?" He answered: "With such devotion, how could our teacher not attain Buddhahood?" Gayata said: "Your teacher is far from the Way. However much and however long he does these practices, it is all only an empty fancy." The disciple asked: "Then by what practice does Your Holiness acquire merit, that you criticize our teacher?" The patriarch replied: "I neither seek the Way nor fall into contrary views, neither humbly worship the Buddha nor become proud, neither practise long meditations nor become neglectful, neither fast nor overeat. I am neither satisfied nor dissatisfied, there is no desire in my mind. This is what is called the Way." He is saying here plainly that it is not a question of seeking the Way, since we already have it, but that perfection is merely to follow it.

There is a poem of Kanzan: "Looking up for the moon in the sky, they lose the jewel which is in their hand." All this is falling into the foolishness of not realizing it is near at hand but seeking it afar. Instead of searching outwardly, search within. The essence of heaven and earth is the same as the essence of self; the universe and I are one, priceless treasure is within. In sum, look down where you stand, attend to where you stand! We must shine our light there and accept gratefully Hakuin's teaching, given like food to starving children, of the futility of looking outside for something that is within.

We all have an ideal which we want to realize, but we must think carefully where we are going to realize that ideal. In a word, we must look for it where we stand and shine our light there. Real peace and eternal happiness, immortality and universal truth, the Way of heaven and earth, in other words the experience of the absolute and infinite, or in religious terms the Buddha way—the great mistake is to think of getting it in some heaven or world on the other side. We never leave the Way for a moment. What we can leave is not the Way. Morning and evening, living and dying, we can never go from it an inch or a second. In China was the brilliant Zen master Joshu, and one day a monk asked him: "What is it, the Way?"

"Outside the fence there," said Joshu immediately. The

way? Oh yes, there it is, outside the fence. But from the monk's side—why no, that's not what I am asking about, that little way outside the fence. The monk says:

"What is it, the Great Way, I mean?" He means the Great Way of the universe. Now Joshu says:

"The great way is the one leading to the capital."

The great way? If it's the great way you mean, that is the road leading to the capital. This will be the main highroad, and in these modern times we can go to the capital by express train. The great way leads to the capital, that was his reply.

Carlyle says: "Nature is the living garment of God." The mountains and rivers, grass and trees which we see before us, this great Nature is the living garment of God. When Goethe saw the fallen leaves forlornly fluttering in the autumn sky, he said: "There is yet force in these very leaves. How should they be dead?" Even those fallen leaves, which make us feel so deeply the sadness of things, have yet a force in them. They have life. How should they be dead? The Vimalakirti Sutra says that the right mind is the place of the Way. Again it is said that the everyday mind is the Way. The everyday mind, the undisturbed mind, as it is, is the Great Way.

All these teach the same thing, that the Way is near and should not be sought afar, that we must look down where we stand and make sure of our ground so that we do not go astray. But people now are too much caught in desire for things, seeing only their own one-sided view, putting their ideals and seeking truth and freedom in non-existent places. Despite all their shifts and twists, the night falls with the Way yet distant. Especially today when the materialist view of Marx dominates the world and people have eyes only for material values, they grasp at the material things in front of them without ever thinking what spirit might be, or what their souls might be. The increase of material desires becomes egotism, becomes opportunism, becomes hedonism, and it is hard to see where the process will stop.

Recently I heard someone discussing the poetry game played by Japanese people at the New Year, which depends on knowing the poems of the famous *Hyakunin Isshu* anthology. In these poems, the ancients adored the moon and the flowers and sought to trace the mysteries of nature in blossoms, birds, wind, snow, and moon. Of course not a few of the verses also sing of human feelings and of love, but always there is delicacy and refinement in them. The modern man, wholly sunk in materialism, an expert in giving nothing away, is hardly one to appreciate such poems. Still, he doesn't want to give up the poetry game, so let us perforce add one more line to make the poems more appropriate to him. And that line (the critic said) can be: "But I want some money too!"

Take the famous poem of Yamabè, the fourth in the anthology:

> I started off along the shore,
> The sea shore at Tago,
> And saw the white and glistening peak
> Of Fuji all aglow
> Through falling flakes of snow.

We put at the end:

> But I want some money too!

Let us try another one:

> I hear the stag's pathetic call
> Far up the mountain side,
> While tramping o'er the maple leaves
> Wind-scattered far and wide,
> This sad, sad autumntide.
> But I want some money too!

Never mind hearing the stag's call and treading on the maple leaves in the deep mountains and feeling sad—if I had some *money* I could go to a pleasure resort and have an

amusing and happy time. But I want some money too! Put
that on the end of each of the poems, and it will just suit the
humour of the modern man.

At the time of the Meiji Restoration in 1868, the abbot of
the Shokokuji temple in Kyoto was Zen master Ekkei. There
was a noted Confucian scholar named Datè whose son later
became foreign minister, and he came to the temple and
saw the abbot: "As you may be aware, I have studied the
Confucian learning, and I have a good understanding of
what the Way is. But as the way of Zen seems to be somewhat different, I have come to ask whether you would be
so good as to tell me something of it." The abbot unexpectedly brought the flat of his hand smack on to the side
of Datè's face. In his surprise and confusion, Datè found
himself outside the room, and the abbot quietly got up,
pulled the door to, and went back to his seat. The samurai
scholar was furious to think of how he had instinctively
fled, and in the corridor stood fingering his sword-hilt,
glaring at the door. A young monk, seeing his threatening
posture, inquired what was the matter. "Why," was the
reply, "nothing at all. Merely an insult from your abbot.
Service under three generations of my feudal lord, and
never anyone dared to lay a finger . . . and now this abbot!
But he can't treat the honour of a samurai like that! I'll
finish him off! . . ." The scowling countenance told that
he meant it. Hearing this, the young monk said he did not
understand it at all but doubtless it would be made clear
later, so would not the guest have tea first? He led the way
to the tea-room, where he poured out a cup for him. Datè
had the tea to his lips and was about to drink when the
monk unexpectedly tapped the arm holding the cup. The
tea spilled over everything. The monk confronted the Confucian and said: "You claimed to have a good understanding
of the Way. Now what is the Way?" Datè tried to find
some phrase from the Four Books or the Five Classics but
failed and hesitated. The other raised his voice: "What is

the Way? Quick, speak, speak!" But he could think of nothing. The monk said: "We have been very rude, but will you be introduced to our Way?" Datè had never come with the intention of being instructed by some young monk like this, but as his own way had failed him he perforce agreed. Then the Zen monk picked up a cloth and mopped up the spilt tea, saying: "This is our Way," and Datè, without thinking, said: "Yes." He had a flash of realization and saw how though he had known in theory that the Way was near at hand and could never be left for a moment, still he had been seeking it afar. He changed his whole thinking and returned to the abbot's room for instruction. After years of intense practice he became a well-known figure in the spiritual history of that time. We should in this way shine the light down to our feet, and so be free to advance or retreat at will, and to act decisively and correctly under that illumination.

One day a flag was fluttering in the breeze before the gate of the temple of the Sixth Patriarch in China. One of the disciples, a man deeply engaged in Zen training, cried: "See how the flag moves today!" Another beside him retorted: "No, today the wind is moving."

"No, it's the flag. Can't you see it actually moving?"

"Not at all, it's the wind. Don't you understand that's the active principle?"

And it developed into a serious dispute. Let me now ask the readers to try the question. In this case what is it that is moving?

Well, the Sixth Patriarch happened to come out, and he told them: "It is not the flag that is moving and not the wind that is moving. It is the mind of the two noble monks." This incident has become one of the koan or classical problems for Zen study, and is called the Case of the Sixth Patriarch and the Wind and the Flag. It is a knotty point. Though the flag be there, if there is no wind it does not move. And though the wind be there, if there is no flag it does not move. Then again, though the flag be there and the wind be there, if there is no observing mind, there is nothing to be called movement. Before the gate there were doubtless cryptomeria and pine trees, but they were not having an argument. There were farmers and woodmen working quietly without minding, and they were not quarrelling. As it happened, in front of the two monks who were moving their minds, the flag was moving.

But it won't do to stop at that and rush away with the idea: "Why yes, of course, it's just the mind that is moving." Even though the two monks do not agitate their minds, the flag without mind is moving. So further, it is not the flag which moves, it is not the wind which moves, it is not even the mind of the two monks. Then what is it that is moving? Let those whose karma has brought them to a reading of this book ponder it and penetrate to the truth.

▪ CHAPTER THREE

The cause of our circling through the six worlds
Is that we are on the dark paths of ignorance.
Dark path upon dark path treading,
When shall we escape from birth-and-death?

THE SONG OF MEDITATION

THESE lines urge the necessity of thinking of liberation. We must not be satisfied with the present condition, living and dying, rising and falling. The path of liberation, of ascension, must be sought. In the Buddhist cosmology there are ten worlds, and the six worlds referred to in the text are the middle and lower ones, namely the worlds of hell, of hungry ghosts, of animals, of demons, of men, and of heaven. The demon world is well known in our folk tales as a place of endless fighting. The four upper worlds are those of Shravakas, Pratyeka Buddhas, Bodhisattvas, and Buddhas. The Buddha world is the peak of enlightenment, and our ideal is to reach that Buddha world. Thus the worlds of all the living beings in the universe are divided into ten; the ten sorts of world are called the ten worlds.

As to circling, just as a wheel turns endlessly, so we are circling in Sansara, now living, now dying, then born again. "Ignorance" is what is technically called in Sanskrit *avidya,* or in Japanese *mumyo,* and it is one of the twelve links in causation. The causes of being born and dying are in Buddhism classified into twelve, and they are the twelve causes of the wheel of life. When they are examined we find the root cause is ignorance, and therefore ignorance or darkness is the first of these causes.

We have here just touched on the formal Buddhist doctrine. Let us go into it a little deeper. Fundamentally the six worlds have no independent existence but are all constructed in one's own mind. From the very beginning we have the Buddha nature, or at least the nature which can attain Buddhahood in the future. But when the black clouds of ignorance arise in the mind, straight away it is born as a demon, or in hell or as a hungry ghost. Good and bad are both what are called "perfumes" in our mind; that is to say, they build up a certain habitual nature. Hell and heaven both, though we do not see them because they are distant from this present world, actually do exist.

The mind is the substance, and the six worlds are the shadow of the mind. When we awaken to this fact and get rid of the karma-obstacles of passion, here and now is the radiant Pure Land world and this very body is the Buddha. Bodhidharma taught this as the first principle of his doctrine in the phrase: "Direct pointing to the heart of man: seeing the nature and becoming Buddha."

Just to recognize these things as logical in theory does not disperse the black clouds in the mind. We have to throw our whole life into practice. The Buddha gave different methods on the principle of suiting the medicine to the disease and teaching according to the capacity of the hearer. Zen has its special methods of catching the mind, bringing under the hammer, living ways and means, and so on. Zen master Hakuin used to hold up one hand in front of the students who flocked to him and say: "Listen to the sound of the single hand!" or "What is the sound of the single hand?" With this he would catch the mind of the students. When the two hands are clapped anyone can hear the sound. But of the one hand, the great soundless sound of the one hand—this is what he forced them to wrestle with.

A form which is visible, a form which has form, can be seen by all, but we have to acquire the eye which can see the formless form. That is sometimes called the single eye; it is the eye of the mind apart from and transcending the physical eye. The eye of the mind must be opened, which can see the truth of heaven and earth, the real meaning of human life. Sometimes Hakuin says: "See your original face." Our present face we can see in a mirror, though not perfectly. But his disciples were forced to try to see that true face, which was before father or mother was born, before heaven and earth were separated. In their struggles they might shed tears of blood, but they were never let off. Nor is this a matter in which one should be easily let off.

Apparently at that time a verse became current which ran something like this:

> *Instead of listening for Hakuin's sound of one hand,*
> *Why not clap both hands and do some business!*

The stall-holders in the street clap their hands to attract attention to their wares and so do trade. But just as Zen has its Zen intuition, has not business also its business intuition? That intuition is something living. The shop or the capital can easily be made over to the children, but the soundless voice, the business instinct—that cannot be explained to them. That secret cannot be handed on, and without it business does not prosper just by shouting or clapping the hands. So let us amend the verse:

> *If you could do business just by clapping the two hands,*
> *Then you need not listen for the sound of the one hand!*

Once the sound of the single hand is heard, once we can see through to the original face, the riddle of the universe is solved then and there. Abbot Ikkyu sings of it:

> *That one who stands wearing the original face,*
> *One glance and beloved for ever.*

Hakuin has three mystical verses:

> *In the black night, when you hear the voice of the black*
> *bird which does not sing—*
> *A father beloved before ever you were born!*

In the depths of the mountains, more remote than Yoshino,
The secret house of the sound of one hand.

Could I but make it heard! On the old temple in the wood
of Shinoda
The sound of the snow falling, late at night.

A special point in Zen is the compassionate way masters like Hakuin demonstrate this wonderful and subtle doctrine, the way to the great peace and the great liberation. Liberation from birth-and-death may sound like a far-off and abstruse conception which does not touch us immediately. But in truth, to get out of birth-and-death, to solve this great problem, is the final object of human life. In Zen it is called the supreme problem, the most pressing of all problems. To resign ourselves to the life of heartbeat and breath, maintaining the body heat and nothing more, is to be merely animal, and no thoughtful human being can be satisfied with it. According to nature and upbringing, the great doubt and questioning will arise in varying forms: Where did we come from into this life, and where do we go after death? What is life? What is death? What after all is the meaning of life? Such questions will arise in some form in everyone. Without solving them we cannot live in peace, cannot sleep in peace, and life becomes agitation and danger. Most of the fever and agony and loneliness of modern life comes from this cause. Meaningless suffering, meaningless distress, fuddled living, and dream-dying. The great thing is to solve the problem of life and death by really living and really dying. To the one who really lives and really dies, life and death disappear. The life without life-and-death is the eternal life. An old verse says:

Having decided on this as the place to which I was finally
bound,
I am happy to live on and on in this body!

But instead of that, people feel:

Oh this world!
Losing and winning and weeping and laughing,
This doing, that doing, and the end all confusion.
And Abbot Ikkyu caps it with a smile:
Oh this world!
Eating and throwing out, sleeping and waking,
And then at the end of it all, only dying!

To transcend life-and-death, to enter the great peace, first it is necessary to get back to the source of the mind.

In the Sutra of Perfect Wisdom, the Buddha tells his disciple Ananda: "You lose sight of the original mind, and seeing the thinking, discriminating mind, take that as your own. But that is not your real mind." Ananda said doubtfully: "By this mind we circle in the six worlds, but by this mind also we attain Buddhahood. If this is not my mind, then how shall I ever attain Buddhahood? Except for this mind, how does one differ from earth and wood and stone?" The Buddha said: "It is not a question of forcibly negating the mind. Now this which you think to be your mind, if it exists, must have a location. Then where is it?" Ananda first said the mind must be inside the body, but the Buddha told him it was not so, and similarly when he said it was outside the body. Pressed further, Ananda suggested seven other locations, but they were not accepted, and finally there was no other place to choose. Then the Buddha said: "The reason that living beings wander beginninglessly in the wheel of birth and death is that they lose the original mind and, seeing the thinking, discriminating mind, take it as their own. Even if they should practise meditation occasionally, while it is on the wrong basis it is erroneous and leads only to lesser wisdom or to darker worlds. The right basis is that which is from the beginning awakened, holy, enlightened, and ever pure. But living beings lose sight of this, their true source. The wrong basis is that which is the beginningless cause of birth and death. As living beings, you all use this latter clinging mind and take it as your real nature; in other words, you believe thinking and discriminating to be the nature of your mind. But if you practise by means of thinking and discriminating you are merely creating new karma, and can no more reach the true source of your being than you can get rice by cooking sand, even for eons of time."

We lose sight of our original mind and take the thinking, discriminating mind as the real mind. This error upon error means the round of the six worlds. If the original mind and original enlightenment are not manifest, then whatever practice we do with the discriminating mind of thoughts and fancies, there is no merit in our labour. The thing is to discard these thoughts and discriminations, and take our stand once more on the original mind of enlightenment. To return to that original enlightenment, the Zen methods are the nearest and quickest.

Modern men prate about rebuilding the world and reforming society. But rebuilding the world can only be done by men who have rebuilt themselves, and the first thing in reforming society is to awaken to one's own self. How to awaken to the real self, how to rebuild the self? Modern men have no interest in "religion." Still, faith in any ideal is a sort of religion, and so the life of idealism can be called a life of religion. Religion is to come out into the true world beyond the sense world, to find the source of human life and understand things from the transcendental standpoint, and live our daily life with that as a basis. Then for the first time as human beings, we can reach a state which the animals cannot reach. And if it is not done, then going forward or going back, we can never escape illusion.

A life of illusion and error is the ghost life. The great teacher who founded the Tendai sect said that we need eyes which can really see and feet by which we can really move. If to that we add a heart with the courage of faith, then we have the three things needed today: eyes which can see truth, feet which grip the ground, and a heart which has faith. One who has not these three is a sort of ghost. With our intellectual education we have increased our intellectual range, but while our heads get stuffed bigger and bigger, our legs wither till we cannot use them. We ignore religion, so we have no faith at heart and have no peace. At least, this is the tendency. People nowadays don't believe in ghosts, but are they not themselves ghosts? "I caught the thief and found it was my own son." What is a ghost? It is a being without seeing eyes, without feet which can move, without faith at heart. Look at the ghosts! Their eyes don't see things as they are but glare fixedly. Their feet cannot grip the ground, and they never get anywhere. They have no faith and so are lost. These are the signs by which to know them:

They have no goal; they are at a loss where to go.

They are lost; their feet cannot hold the ground, and they drift about the world.

They are malignant; their voices are full of hate of themselves and others.

Isn't this just the picture of modern man?

Religion is not only the key-note of spiritual life, but at the same time its source. Of the right mind it is not only the refuge and protection, but also the nourishment. It is only through this function of religion as an inspiration to the mind that our civilization, in politics, economics, ethics, education, and the rest, has reached its present stage. Religion has been the mainspring of all. It is beyond these things and yet is the principle of their growth. True religion is the height of human culture. A culture without it is only a lifeless shell. Modern man is not concerned with religion because he does not know what religion is, but the result is a whittling away of his life as an individual. Religion does not exist for its own sake, but to give light and meaning to our life. It is to light the dark paths, to transcend life-and-death, to give immortality.

That illumination, that life beyond life-and-death, does have compassion on those in the round of the six paths, with their darkness and suffering. But as Muso Kokushi says: "When we look at people today, they are piling up wrong thinking day and night, and outwardly too doing only evil. Yet they pray of course to gods and Buddhas for good luck, and ask that their lives, just as they are, should be prolonged. When the prayer is made in such a spirit, how should it be answered? Day and night disobeying all gods and Buddhas, and then they resent it that their prayers are not granted." The old verse runs:

When in the praying heart there is no sincerity,
The prayer gets the answer of no answer.

Contrary and clinging attachments born of folly are the cause of wandering in the worlds; from foolishness greed arises, from greed anger is born—by these three we are tormented.

When one wish is met, then there is a second,
A third, fourth, fifth. . . . O sixfold difficult world!

In Buddhism there are what are called the four sufferings, and another classification of eight sufferings. The four sufferings are birth, old age, sickness, and death, and to them are added the second four: meeting with what is painful, seeking and not finding, separation from what is loved, and the sufferings arising at maturity. We can understand that age, sickness, and death should be sufferings, but it seems hard to see why birth should be accounted a suffering. Still, inasmuch as it gives rise to the other three, it can be regarded so. As to the sufferings from maturity of body and mind— well, most of the sufferings of our daily life are contained under this head.

This world is said to be a place of suffering. But in fact there are none in it who suffer as human beings suffer, and among human beings those who think and discriminate more suffer correspondingly. For instance, when a house is supposed to be haunted, however alarming the story may be, the dogs and cats and infants and half-wits who cannot understand are not upset by it. Nor of course is a Buddha or Bodhisattva. It is just the human beings in the middle who are frightened by the illusory creation of the mind. Still, the capacity to be deluded, to suffer, means also the capacity to be enlightened, to have bliss. The earth which gives rise to the weeds can also nourish the grain. A desert is not plagued by weeds, but that fact proves that wheat will not grow there either. So it can be said that to be deluded and to suffer is the prerogative of human beings. Then we have to seize the opportunity, whenever it comes, for a mental revolution which will knock away the block that impedes realization. Hakuin is urging us in the Song to use the chance. If we can take away the wedge that prevents the turning-over in the mind, then the four contrary views will immediately be converted into the four virtues of Nirvana. Sansara is Nirvana; the passions are the bodhi. Sansara is no longer an agony for us, and more than that, we can vivify Sansara and the world about us is changed.

■ CHAPTER FOUR

> *The Zen meditation of the Mahayana*
> *Is beyond all our praise.*

THE SONG OF MEDITATION

THESE two lines are the central pivot of the Song of Meditation. Mahayana is a Sanskrit word meaning "great vehicle." Hakuin here refers to meditation, which is the peak of the Mahayana, or Buddhism of the Great Vehicle. When it is experienced, the darkness of ignorance clears up of itself, the spiritual light of realization of truth appears, and endless blessings are manifested. There are four famous phrases attributed to Bodhidharma:

> *Direct pointing to the human heart;*
> *Seeing the nature and becoming Buddha;*
> *Not standing on letters;*
> *A separate transmission outside the scriptures.*

The direct pointing to the heart of man leads to seeing the nature and becoming Buddha. It cannot be written in letters or taught in scriptures; transmission from heart to heart is the basis of Bodhidharma's Zen.

An important point to notice first is that though there are innumerable paths in Buddhism suited to the different circumstances of the people, they can be broadly classified under the paths of the Great Vehicle and those of the Small Vehicle. The former are said to be for those in whom wisdom is already to some extent manifest, and the latter for those who have not yet attained it. Zen or meditation again is of different kinds: there is Zen of the mystics outside Buddhism, there is Zen of the Small Vehicle schools, there is the ordinary man's Zen, and there is also bogus Zen. But here we are speaking of the highest peak, Mahayana Zen, of which it is said that it is peerless and beyond all praise. The darkness clears, and the blessings become manifest of themselves. As to these blessings, the Song will refer to them later, but the real virtue of Zen meditation, its special glory, must be what is called wisdom-power. Wisdom-power is not something miraculous, but it means things being what they really are, that we see them as they really are and handle them as they really are.

To see everything as it truly is, and to bring it to life and use it in absolute freedom. It doesn't mean those old stories of miracles like the legendary colt coming out of the wine gourd, or the world being made in seven days, or a baby being born from the side of the mother. These things are supposed to be examples of spiritual power, but to take them as such is a big mistake. In the truth there is nothing miraculous. The spiritual power of Zen means to live in the ordinary way all day, but without any check or hindrance, bright as a mirror is bright, smoothly as a ball running across a tray, without any sticking or hanging back. As when the ice is melted there is no congealing or stiffness, so the man of realization lives an ordinary life, but with infinite freedom, released from all restrictions.

The secret of seeing things as they are is to take off our coloured spectacles. That being-as-it-is, with nothing extraordinary about it, nothing wonderful, is the great wonder. The ability to see things normally is no small thing, to be really normal is unusual. In that normality begins to bubble up inspiration. When rarely by chance a deformed child is born, many people wonder at it, and there is a great to-do among the neighbours. (Of course nothing is really chance.) But in a way it is equally unusual when something hardly ever happens or it hardly ever doesn't happen. It is even more wonderful that millions of men, without any blue-print from anyone, are born in the same human form. When we can see the great wonder where there is nothing "wonderful," when we can see the great beauty in the unbeautiful, everything begins to radiate spiritual light. Zen gives spiritual flavour to everyday food and drink in the same way that the popular Aji-no-moto essence is used in every family to bring out the flavour of our food. As a matter of fact, it is not so much that Zen gives flavour to things; the things have that taste of Zen, that seed of infinity, already in them. It is only necessary to see things with the Zen eye. The poor painter gets the shape and form right, but cannot, as they say, paint the flowers so that we smell them or paint the waterfall so that we hear it. It is Zen which gives scent and sound to the picture of the universe and brings everything to life.

The Emperor Koshu of the Southern Sung dynasty asked Zen master Engo Kokugon about the peak of Zen attainment, and he replied; "When the emperor with benevolence and piety maintains the peace, every corner of the empire enjoys illumination. Grass, trees, and insects too have each their place. This is the way transmitted by Buddhas and patriarchs, and apart from this there is no other way. If there should be some other way, it is not the way of the Buddhas and patriarchs." When the emperor rules with benevolence and piety, the people become sincere and loyal in carrying out their duties, and the empire can be at peace. In this is the savour of life, in this is the scent. Modern men have forgotten this clear way, the normal natural way, and there arise confusion and fever and unrest. The way of Zen teaches spiritual action of the mind-essence, the ability to see heaven and earth as they really are, and then heaven and earth become radiant, and paradise appears.

As to how the secret is to be discovered, there is a suggestive passage of question and answer in the No play called *Hoka So* (The Renunciate Priests), in which the two brothers, as priests, are asked about Zen.

"From what patriarch do the renunciate priests receive their Zen? I would hear the doctrine of your sect."

"Our doctrine is a special transmission outside the scriptures, and though we speak, it remains unspoken. It is not taught by teaching; to produce words and phrases is to fall into scripture-making; to take a stand on letters is to betray the doctrine. But from the fluttering of a leaf you can know the movement of the wind."

"Truly this is interesting. And what of the koan of zazen?"

"Going within, to plumb the abyss; going out, to delight in Samadhi."

"And of the doctrine that this body is the Buddha?"

"Where the white clouds are thick, the golden dragon sports."

"If we dwell in life-and-death? . . ."

"The round of suffering."

"And as to the road aloft?"

"Cut all to pieces!"

Here there is a brief break connected with the action of the plot, but the speaker continues later:

"Not to lament, whether the root or stem be great or small;

Not to choose whether the law be kept or broken;

Not to fall into either being or not being—

This is the sign by which all become Buddhas."

Zen is not a picture of a thing but confronting the thing itself. It is not a theoretical conclusion but grasping reality. The Sixth Patriarch in one of his discourses says: "What is zazen or sitting-in-meditation? On this path there are no obstacles or impediments. In the outer world of good and evil, when not a thought arises in the mind, that is called za (sitting). Inwardly to see one's own nature and not be moved, that is called Zen (meditation).

"What is called Zenjo (meditation and Samadhi)? Without, to be separated from form, is called Zen; within, to

7. FUJI FROM MOUNT SHAKA, BY OKA KYUGAKU.
Above the clouds the monk is at ease on the Buddha mountain, and the Absolute, symbolized here by the peerless Mount Fuji, reveals itself before him.

have no disturbance, is called Samadhi. If outwardly we stick to a form then the mind is disturbed, and if we are separated from form the mind is not disturbed. The original nature is naturally pure and naturally in Samadhi, but to be consciously seeing that state is itself a disturbance. If in witnessing any state the mind does not move, this is the real Samadhi. Without, to be separated from form is already Zen; within, not to be disturbed is already Samadhi; outward Zen and inward Samadhi—this is Zen."

The Sutra of the Net of Brahma has an interesting passage: "The original nature is from the beginning naturally pure. If in the midst of all thoughts we see the original nature as pure, then by this natural discipline and natural practice, the Buddha way is naturally accomplished."

The Sixth Patriarch, when asked about Zen, replied: "Without thinking of good, without thinking of evil, now what is your original face?" When we can perceive directly that original face, we attain the secret of Zen naturally. The Sixth Patriarch forces on us the necessity of grasping the original "I," or what is philosophically called the inmost true Self.

The "sound of one hand" is a koan devised by Hakuin himself. Essentially this koan, and the Sixth Patriarch's "original face," are intended to smash the basis of our common-sense experience which relies on logic. A fundamental breaking up is essential for establishing the new spiritual Zen outlook. The original face sounds as if it might be something seen with the eye, and the sound of one hand something rather to be heard, but their ultimate object is the same. It is that we may open the secret storehouse of the mind and obtain the inexhaustible treasure in it. Verily the sound of the one hand is resounding through heaven and earth and beyond; the original face is resplendent before heaven and earth are separated, and after space itself ceases to exist.

Zen is the supreme product of Far Eastern culture, but

the one thing on which it prides itself is the systematic training of the mind, to manifest the secret and so attain realization. Its system and training (and also the final attainment) take a different form from those of other mystical schools. In particular it has the special methods of zazen and koan. Of course to practise zazen, or to wrestle with a koan, may not be absolutely essential to realization, but these are the quickest and the surest methods.

What is obtained by practising Zen? It cannot be acquiring something which is not already possessed. All that can be said is that, as to himself, he sees and realizes that "the eyes are on each side and the nose in the middle," and as to the world, he sees directly that the flowers are red and the willows green. The world changes. I catch the thief and find it is my own son. The demon of yesterday now is coming to pray. Zen master Rinzai tells us: "Not being tainted by life-and-death, free in action, not seeking anything special, it is attained of itself." Purity and freedom, the experience of non-egoity, are revealed.

Abbot Daiko of Daitokuji temple made a painting of a *hyotan* or wine-gourd and on it wrote this poem:

> *O buoyant one! Not of true melon rank,*
> *Not fresh and cool to eat like your cousin the water-melon,*
> *Yet you are light, being emptied of desires,*
> *And the mountain sages make you their companion,*
> *Fill you with wine and carry you at their waist.*
> *You brought forth the colt in the fairy story—'twas your sport;*
> *Though of melon suit, you do not suffer under the kitchen knife—'tis your wisdom;*
> *When with you they try to catch the slippery catfish, you let it escape—'tis your benevolence;*
> *You were the badge on the horse of great Hideyoshi—'tis your bravery.*
> *Are you not praiseworthy?*

The freedom of non-egoity must also be attached to spiritual action:

Even the wine gourd which lives life so lightly,
Has a cord tied round its waist to hold it.

Zen is called the peerless doctrine of the Buddhas, the teaching that spiritualizes all, the Buddha-heart doctrine, the teaching of the source of the mind. As it is the holy way of all the Buddhas, it is the way of liberation for us. Wisdom is the root of it, and compassion the conclusion. The spiritual action which brings all to spirituality, to goodness, to virtue, cannot be expressed by pen or tongue or thought, but is something that has to be experienced for oneself.

In olden times the T'ang Emperor Koso asked of a sage who was practising the Way in the mountains: "You are always living in the depths of the mountains. What happiness is there in such places?" To which the man of the mountains replied in a verse:

What is there in the mountains?
In the mountains the white clouds are many.
But this is something you have to enjoy by coming your-
self.
I cannot take them and present them to you.

"What is the happiness in the mountains?" asks the emperor. "Why, Your Majesty, in the mountains are those long-sought white clouds. Morning and evening they wrap me round and bring serenity to my heart. But this joy is mine alone, because it is something that has to be experienced for oneself. Ah, the white clouds! I should like to put them in a box and present them to you, but it cannot be done. They cannot be caught and given to another, so unfortunately. . . ." With these words he brings out clearly the disadvantages of high rank. Confucius also pointed to independence and not being under the control of another, when he said: "Eating coarse food and drinking water, with the bent elbow for a pillow—there is yet happiness in these things."

What was the origin of Zen? Long ago when the Buddha

was with the assembed listeners on Vulture Peak, a great Brahmin offered him a golden flower which he took and in silence showed to the assembly. Among the eighty thousand men and gods none took his meaning except Kashyapa, whose face broke into a smile. The Buddha at once said: "I have the treasure of the eye of the true doctrine, the spiritual heart of Nirvana, the great truth that the real form is no form; and now it is with Kashyapa." So it was transmitted to Kashyapa, from heart to heart, teacher and pupil face to face. Such was the beginning of Zen. Buddhist sects in India and later in China and Japan take their stand on the scriptures and have each their authoritative texts, but Zen alone has no special text, for it transmits the Buddha heart which cannot be expressed in a text, and so it is also called the Buddha-heart sect. From Shakyamuni Buddha to Kashyapa, Kashyapa to Ananda in succession, at last it reached the twenty-eighth Bodhidharma. He carried it to China, where he became the First Patriarch, the second being Eka, the third Sosan, the fourth Doshin, the fifth Konin, and the sixth Eno. It came later to Japan where it was handed down, and one line came to Hakuin.

We have to really study and really go into the meaning of the flower and the smile in the assembly on the mountain. Not Zen alone, but beauty in any form makes words fail. Many are the poems and songs about the beauty of the cherry-blossoms of Yoshino, and the landscape of Matsu-shima, but the best, which express the supreme beauty most perfectly, are these:

> "This, oh this!"
> Was all I could say,
> Before the flowers of Yoshino.

And of Matsushima:

> Matsushima!
> Ah, Matsushima! Matsushima!

There is no way of telling about beauty. Even if we manage to say something it falls short.

> To the one who has not seen,
> What shall I say
> Of the shore of Suma?
> For when one sees it
> One can find no words.

So the Mahayana meditation is beyond all our praise, because there are no words. Call it spiritual flavour, spiritual way, wonderful principle, or wonderful law, the essence of holy teaching—but it is the absolute state where the four statements are left behind and the hundred negations excluded, where words end and the working of the mind is extinguished *(Plate 7)*. This state has to be known in oneself by oneself. Yet it is not something difficult, not something hidden, not something distant. Before one's eyes, by one's side, clearly it is revealed in its purity and majesty. Let us open our eyes. It is only opening the eyes. The poem of realization by Sotoba runs:

> The sound of the valley stream is His great tongue,
> The colours of the mountains are His pure body.
> In the night I have heard the eighty-four thousand hymns,
> But how to tell the people the next day?

After long years of training, going deeper into Zen without relapsing, one day realization appears, and this poem expresses the experience of that moment. The voice of the waterfall is the great sermon of the Buddha, the colours of those mountains are the Buddha's pure truth-body *(Plate 8)*. Throughout the night is the unbroken sermon of the truth-body teaching the eighty-four thousand gates of the Law. Alas, that peak of joy, that state of bliss cannot be expressed or told to others. How sublime the teaching, how noble the truth! And the water of that doctrine is bathing us, the flowers of that truth are blooming in profusion before our eyes. The way is near, the thing is easy. "Look down where you stand!" is the spear-thrust of the Zen master.

One day Bodhidharma said to his disciples that the day had come for him to return to India, and told each to bring

8. MOUNTAINS AND GORGES, BY TAKASHINA ROSEN.
"The sound of the valley stream is His great tongue,
The colours of the mountains are His pure body." (See opposite.)

forward what he had to offer. Dofuku said: "As I see it, it is not employing words nor abandoning them, but directly using the Way." A high view indeed.

Bodhidharma said: "You have my skin."

The nun Soji said: "As I understand it, it is as when Ananda had a vision of the paradise of the Buddha of the East; it appeared and then vanished." This is also a noteworthy view.

Bodhidharma said: "You have my flesh."

Doiku said: "The four great elements are empty, and the five aggregates non-existent. According to my view, there is nothing to be obtained; words and phrases are cut off and the working of the mind disappears." This is a high transcendental view.

Bodhidharma said: "You have my bones."

Last came Eka, who just stood before the master, made a reverence, and went back to his place without a word of discussion or any phrase presenting his view. As we picture him standing in the state of no-mind, coming before the teacher, bowing his head, and then quietly resuming his place, what can be said? I cannot restrain my tears of reverence for him. He indeed had attained the end.

Bodhidharma said: "You have my marrow." With these words he invested him with the succession as the Second Patriarch in China.

We are ceaselessly restless for some truth or absolute. We yearn to discover some god or Buddha. But in fact, which one of those four disciples of Bodhidharma is our own state? Is it not true that we do not even have the skin? To get pure water one must dig deeply and not go wandering about.

In the Vimalakirti Sutra there is a discussion on non-duality, and in it the story of Vimalakirti's "silence like thunder." What the sutra calls non-duality is the main point of Buddhism, the essence of the sutras and the peak of Mahayana. Non-dual means not two. By non-duality,

duality is resolved and becomes not two. But it is not that it becomes altogether one. Two but not two, one but not one, two and yet one, one and yet two, it can be called neither one nor two. Distinctions are themselves sameness, sameness is itself distinctions—this is the truth of the universe. To experience that truth is the object of Mahayana meditation. In the sutra there is a discussion on non-duality among the Bodhisattvas. Thirty-one of them put forward their views, and finally Manjushri, the Bodhisattva of Wisdom, was asked to speak. He said: "As to the truth of things, what can be said? For there are no words. If it were taught in words, the truth would be obscured. The world of truth cannot be expressed by words." The whole company turned to Vimalakirti and entreated him with his matchless eloquence to express the truth of non-duality. All listened with strained attention for him to speak. He closed his mouth firmly and would not open it. There was only silence. Yet this was a great expression of truth, beyond all words, and it became famous as Vimalakirti's "silence like thunder." Verily throughout the ages the great teaching of non-duality is reverberating through heaven and earth. Never is the Way two; to the master the Way is one only.

■ CHAPTER FIVE

Giving and morality and the other perfections,
Taking of the Name, repentance, discipline,
And the many other right actions,
All come back to the practice of meditation.

THE SONG OF MEDITATION

IN THESE lines the right actions are reviewed, and it is taught that the Zen meditation of the Mahayana is the highest of them. It is the peak of the Mahayana, so great, so profound, that all merit comes back to it. The master of the Zuiganji temple at Matsushima, famous for its scenery, wrote a poem which became well-known:

Beneath the skies there are mountains and streams;
Each has one kind of beauty for its own.
But those beauties all come back to the beauty of Matsu-
shima—
Beneath the skies there are no other mountains and streams.

It is like this with the Mahayana Zen meditation. To say that all other right actions come back to it may seem like a vulgar boast of the Zen sect. But Hakuin had no sectarian narrowness in him, and he is teaching from the standpoint of the whole Mahayana. When he says that all deeds of merit go back to Zen meditation, his meaning is that they cannot exist without it. Unless they have this as their root and spring from this, they have no real meaning. All true acts of merit are included in meditation; it is their parent and they are born from it. Zen master Shoichi says: "Meditation is the way to the great liberation. All righteousness flows from it; all the actions find their consummation here;

wisdom and divine inspiration are born from it; the life of man and of heaven derives from it." And again: "What is called Zen is the Buddha heart. Morality is its outer form; taking the Name is a means to it. Their Samadhi all comes from the Buddha heart. For this reason the Zen practice is the root of the others."

Hakuin refers to giving and morality and the other perfections. There are six perfections of the Bodhisattva, but these and the practice of the Name and the other meritorious deeds all go back to meditation. Or rather, when they come from meditation, then alone they are truly deeds of merit. In the *Shodoka* poem of Yoka Daishi, he says:

When suddenly he awakens to the Buddha's Zen,
The six perfections and the ten thousand right actions are
found perfect within him.

Although the act be the same, if the basis is wrong and the source tainted, what is normally a particularly good action may become no good action at all. It becomes hypocrisy, a trick, nothing at all. In the Zen phrase, water drunk by the cow becomes milk, and drunk by the snake becomes poison. The same water becomes in the former pure milk and benefits others, and in the latter a terrible poison and harms others. This is a significant statement.

The six perfections are: giving, morality, endurance, energy, meditation (Zen), and wisdom. The Sanskrit word for such perfection is *paramita*, which means attaining the far shore. The sense is that of leaving this shore of illusion and attaining the further shore of enlightenment; leaving this shore of empirical experience and attaining the far shore of the ideal. The boat of the perfections crosses the great river between the two shores. The practice of the six perfections is essential for the Bodhisattva to attain Buddhahood. Bodhisattva means in Sanskrit one whose mind is in enlightenment. He has awakened from the dream of illusions; he treats the interests of others as his own; above, he seeks wisdom, and below, he engages himself in helping all.

This is a special being, advanced on the path of wisdom, who nevertheless turns to labour in every way for the good of all. So we too must rouse in ourselves the Bodhisattva spirit of aspiration combined with service.

The first perfection is giving. It has not just the superficial and narrow meaning of contributing money to some temple, as people think. It means practice of benevolence, love, compassion, and virtue, and is of three kinds: giving things, giving truth by teaching, and giving fearlessness by inspiring another with courage and strength.

The second perfection is morality or conduct which avoids the wrong and performs the right. This is the foundation of human life, and without it no one can live as he should. There are five commandments binding on all, monks and laymen alike:

> Not to kill: to protect the life of living things.
> Not to steal: to respect the distinction between one's own and another's, and what is for all and what is private.
> Not to commit adultery: to abstain from wantonness.
> Not to lie: to keep words and actions in consonance.
> Not to become intoxicated: always to keep the mind composed.

These five can be reduced to three: to abstain from wrong, to do right, and to exert oneself for the world and other people.

The third perfection is endurance. It means the strong fortitude by which one can be patient whether things go well or against him.

The fourth perfection is energy, which is sustained exertion, a spirit which never turns back.

The fifth is Zen meditation, which means silencing the thought and looking within. The word is the same, but this perfection of Zen meditation *(Zenjo)* is just one of the six perfections and so distinct from the others, whereas the

Mahayana Zen meditation is something absolute, and includes all perfections.

The sixth perfection is wisdom, the power of clear penetration. In Sanskrit the word is *prajna,* and the perfection of wisdom is *prajnaparamita,* which is seeing all things and the truth behind them, as they really are. The six perfections are the great principles, the great virtues, without which we cannot live as real men. The path of the Bodhisattva is the path of a real man. Let us set out the perfections from this point of view.

Giving: that we join together for mutual help.

Morality: that we join together to preserve the social order.

Endurance: that we remain strong in patience in the face of anything that comes.

Energy: that we work in earnest at the task before us.

Zen meditation: that we attain unshakable conviction.

Wisdom: that we act on a right view of the things of the world.

Hakuin mentions taking the holy Name, repentance, and discipline. *Nembutsu* or taking the holy Name of Buddha can be either mental repetition of the Name or audible repetition. The Nembutsu of the self-power schools is mainly mental, by Zen meditation looking to the Buddha or Bodhisattva within and turning in prayer to him. In the Nembutsu of the other-power schools, the holy Name is repeated audibly. Since it is endowed with all virtues and right actions, the man repeating it naturally receives the Buddha wisdom and becomes a Buddha. Whether mentally or verbally, the mere taking of the Name is of great spiritual efficacy.

I will add here a word about self-power and other-power. There are those who think of them as opposed to each other and incompatible. But fundamentally the Way can never be two. The culmination of faith is the experience in which the Buddha and oneself become one. In bringing about this oneness, the other-power school puts the Buddha on that side, and then by the power of the holy Name leaves this side and enters the Buddha, becoming one with him. In the self-power school, we first purify our own hearts by Zen meditation, and then invite the Buddha to this side to become one with us. There is the formal distinction between going and receiving, but as the host and guest become identified there is no real difference. From the point of view of the world of form, for us to go there is not the same as inviting the Buddha here, but in the formless world there cannot be any difference between them. We must know that the Samadhi of oneness is the goal of faith.

Now as to repentance, which means to correct our past wrong-doing. It is very important in the spiritual life, and there is no religious school that does not lay stress on it. Repentance is one of the glories of religion, so much so that one could say that apart from religion there is no real repentance.

The six perfections such as giving and morality, and the taking of the Name and repentance and discipline and so many other good actions of great spiritual value, all come back to the Zen meditation of the Mahayana. Or rather, they are born of it.

Looking at the world today, one would like to urge at least just the practice of giving. So many people simply want to get from others, to take or even to rob; they hardly think of giving, of being kind, of helping. With this attitude it is very illogical to expect peace and prosperity. If we want to get, let us first give; nay, to give for the sake of getting is already only utilitarianism. The perfection of giving is to give what one has—the wealthy to give money, the wise to give wisdom, the strong to give their strength. Until the day when we become true givers we need not hope for real peace or success in life. But these days the rich man keeps his capital, and the man of education makes that education his capital, and the strong man makes that strength *his* capital, and they all use it to try to make a profit out of others. A real giver would not consider his means, but would practise giving at any time and place. The merit in a gift is not necessarily proportionate to the value of the gift or the amount. The old saying is, better the single light of the poor man than the thousand lamps of the rich man. The merit lies only in the sincerity. The principle of giving is to give joyfully from a feeling of sympathy, free from any desire for name or a return of some kind. And if there is nothing to give? If the circumstances do not permit us to give, then let us rejoice in a gift made by others. Such rejoicing at the welfare of the receiver of the gift is declared by the sutras to surpass in merit even giving itself. Surely at least we can be glad at the happiness of another?

Which would we prefer, a simple cup of tea offered with sincerity, or dainties of mountain and ocean served with vulgar ostentation or as business entertainment? Surely the tea. The trouble is that as soon as they hear this, people think that they may as well never serve anything but just a cup of tea—with full sincerity of course—instead of going to all the trouble of making a meal for the guests! Economically it would have many advantages—a sort of austerity programme when business is not too good—so why not kill two birds with one stone and take up this "tea-ism"? But the man who can put real sincerity into serving a cup of tea is the very man who will do everything possible besides. O people of today! Rich man, influential man, clever man, strong man—be ready each to give what you have for the good of all. Or at least when you see others giving, do not begrudge it in your hearts. That society where people know how to give will have perfect peace and prosperity.

While we are subject to the passions of the three poisons and the five desires, our giving and morality and the other perfections, our taking of the Name and repentance and discipline and the other good deeds, are only a fair form and have no real meaning. This is why we must bring them back to the Zen meditation. For instance, there are various ways of taking the Name, or Nembutsu as it is technically called. A young man criticized his grandmother, who used to recite the formula of the holy Name, *Namu Amida Butsu* (reverence to Amitabha Buddha):

> *Morning and evening the Name is clearly heard,*
> *But all mixed up with nagging—what an empty Nembutsu!*

The old lady came back at him:

> *Morning and evening the Nembutsu is for the ear of the*
>   *holy Buddha,*
> *The scoldings with it are for the family!*

What a pair!

How different from Saint Shinran's "The repetition of the Name may cause me to fall into hell; the repetition of the Name may cause me to enter paradise. Shinran is not concerned with either."

Saint Ippen, when he was training under his teacher, was given the mantra *Namu Amida Butsu* as a koan. He practised the Samadhi of the Nembutsu and then presented his view to the teacher in this verse:

> *When I recite it, there is neither myself nor Buddha;*
> *Namu Amida Butsu—only the voice remains.*

The teacher did not give his approval to this, and Ippen plunged himself again in his spiritual exercises. Then he produced another verse:

> *When I recite it, there is neither myself nor Buddha;*
> *Namu Amida Butsu, Namu Amida Butsu!*

Tradition says this verse was approved. In either verse the first line is well, but if we say the voice remains then the existence of the voice means a distinction between the man who recites the name and the Buddha whose name is recited, and real Samadhi is yet far away. In the second version, the object and the self have become one in Samadhi. Yet another last line has been proposed:

When I recite it, there is neither myself nor Buddha;
The water-bird is splashing in the water of the pond.
This too has a flavour of its own.

The essence of human life is not robbing each other but helping, not dictatorship but mutual aid. People who can give cheerfully, quietly, with a friendly smile, are people whose life has a meaning. "Fortune enters through the smiling gate." The one who can live with a smile, without needing any fortune coming from elsewhere, is himself the god of fortune. Compared with this how tasteless is modern life—restless, discontented, and yet sluggish.

Irritable, easily angered, and always in a bad humour, dissatisfied with oneself and persecuting others, what can be worse than this sort of life? The sutras warn us how the fire of anger can burn up a forest of merit; though our merits and right actions are piled high as a mountain, one flash of anger can burn them all up. Wrath is the most terrible thing in the world. Hakuin wrote a short essay on anger in which he says: "That man in whom the truth is bright has no anger. When truth is obscured, anger arises. Mostly it arises when we are crossed, and ceases when our desires are met. In the world all is as it should be. If one crosses me, it is my own fault; there is already a fault in myself. How should I ignore the fault in myself and become angry at him? When I am angry with him, my fault is doubled." It is rightly said. To become angry is to proclaim one's mental darkness, to expose one's fault.

Still, joy and anger, grief and pleasure are instinctive feelings, and it must be admitted they are hard to suppress. Then instead of directing our anger outwards we should direct it inwards and turn it on ourselves. Let us rage and storm at our own ineffective snivelling, at our sins, at our stupidity. In olden days Abbot Jimyo, sitting in meditation day and night through the bitter winter, found himself often invaded by the demon of sleep. He took a gimlet and drove it into his thigh with the words: "The light of the ancient sages was made great through piercing sufferings. Alive to achieve nothing, and to die unknown to any, what use is such a life?" Is this not a moving story? To turn the anger within is the foundation of noble achievement.

Again, if we are to be angry, then let us put aside mere peevishness or feminine tantrums and be really angry. It is said that the philosopher-sage Mencius only once became angry, but then the whole country was pacified. In Japanese history there is the case of the Emperor Meiji, who became angry only once, but then he assumed command of the armed forces and at once established peace. In Chinese history is the well-known case of the humble and modest Rin Shojo, who went as envoy to confront the tyrant, and in his anger took unopposed and brought back the stolen jade.

Nevertheless, such cases are few, and anger generally means failure. In ordinary life we should not proclaim our own stupidity, but consider our shortcomings and be magnanimous and patient. In the Upasaka Sutra or sutra for laymen it is said: "Patient endurance is the real cause of enlightenment. The Anuttara-samyak-sambodhi or peerless wisdom is the fruit of this patience." Another sutra says that the man who can practise patient endurance is the real hero. Anger finally turns into hatred, into jealousy, into cursing against life, and there is no knowing where its poison will stop. It is a fearful thing. There are some old songs of the Way:

When the other draws the sword of injustice,
Let it come to rest in the sheath of one's own heart.

Though hated, do not return hate,
For hating and hating again there will be no end.

Look! The rice assailed by fire and water
Is patient, and becomes cooked.

Oh that sigh!

> *It is a carpenter's plane*
> *That pares away your life.*

Patient endurance is gold. A patient man has courage to bear whatever comes. Nowadays people lack patience; they are always saying they cannot go *through* with things. And this restlessness and discontent is the enemy of happiness and success. The people are cherishing mistaken grudges against each other and are uneasy with each other. Thus they invite sufferings. The old saying is, make difficulties thy treasure; work and patience are the foundation of success.

There is a ray of hope even for a country in ruins. In the very abyss of despair there is the gleam of a jewel. Without tribulation of body and mind a good knight will hardly be made; without manure a good crop will hardly grow; without fatigue in all the limbs the work will hardly be done well; without contesting every point a good bargain will hardly be obtained.

There is a painting by Zen master Sengai, in his usual unconventional style and splendid brushwork, showing a man in the prime of life with his shoulders high and eyes aglare, a picture of fury. To this he has written a poem: "Anger is the great treasure of thy house. Hide it deep and do not bring it out recklessly." Anger must be our jewel, our great treasure. Surely it must be locked safely in the depths of the vault. If necessary, once a year it may be looked at for an airing. But to bring a diamond into the kitchen to cut up the vegetables is a misuse of something precious, and displays total lack of understanding. There is another old picture which shows merely a perfect circle, and the poem reads:

> *The rounded pearl of thy character—*
> *Let it have one irregularity.*
> *If quite round, it will roll too easily.*

When we accept life and the truth behind life and put down our anger, turning it within to spur us on, when we go forward in patience, there is peace in all the worlds. For yesterday, forgetting; for today, rejoicing; for tomorrow, bliss. Or as the Zen saying is, satisfaction with the past, gratitude for the present, and spiritual energy for the future. This is the spiritual attitude to the three states of time. The power of the Zen meditation of the Mahayana is necessary as the basis so that we can live our every day like this.

CHAPTER SIX

By the merit of a single sitting
He destroys innumerable accumulated sins.
How should there be wrong paths for him?
The Pure Land paradise is not far.

THE SONG OF MEDITATION

THESE lines speak of the virtue of sitting-in-meditation, and especially in regard to repentance and the destruction of sins. The Sixth Patriarch, explaining the word zazen or sitting-in-meditation, says: "In the outer world of good and evil, when not a thought arises in the mind, that is called za (sitting); inwardly, to see one's own nature and not be moved, that is called Zen (meditation)." The "wrong paths" of the verse are those which lead ultimately to reincarnation as a dweller in hell, as a ghost, or as an animal. If the meditation practice is really done, then the merits are as great as declared in the Song. The important thing in practising Zen is not so much the length or shortness of the time, but that the mind should be in a state where the meditation is steady and continuous. When it is said that those who perform meditation for even one session destroy innumerable accumulated sins, it means that if this meditation goes into the real Samadhi, then a single session has this great power. One session means a single sitting, as when we set up a stick of incense and do not leave our meditation till it has burnt down.

There are directions for the practice. In a place, which must be quiet, lay a thick cushion and seat yourself on it in an upright posture. First swell out the "field of the elixir" *(tanden)*, namely the abdomen below the navel, and put your strength there. Let the shoulders be directly below the ears, and the navel below the nose. Make the spine straight. The mouth should be shut and the eyes slightly opened. The breath should flow gently. In this correct posture, meditate on the koan which you have been given, or in the case of beginners practise counting the breaths. By this last method dull and distracted thought is eliminated. Then, entering the Samadhi of undisturbed purity, remain in meditation. Those who are really determined should look at the small classic called *Zazen-gi* for the details of the method.*

Of course it may be that there are those whose insight and inner nature are so advanced that they would not necessarily require to practise exactly in the way described, but still there are many advantages in beginning in the orthodox manner. If the practice is truly carried out, one session of meditation is one session of Buddha; a day of meditation is a day of Buddha. Or as an ancient has said: "One inch of meditation, one inch of Buddha; so inch by inch, to the six-foot form of Buddha."

If we do our meditation practice properly, then the up-rising thoughts, though they be the sins and impediments accumulated for eons past, will be extinguished of themselves, and then where should the wrong paths be? The Pure Land paradise is not far. We enter the state where this very body is the Buddha. The thing to be kept in mind for meditation is the great conviction that this is the path that can save us, and it is only this path that can save us. The attitude of trying just to see what it is like, or as an experiment, is not appropriate in such a serious business. Underneath the great faith you will come upon the great questioning, and then if you whip up your efforts with great determination and rush on ahead, below the great

* These details are given in Chapters II and III of *A Tongue-tip Taste of Zen.*

questioning there is found the great realization, and without any doubt know that you will have it.

Apart from attaining full realization, to be able to sit quiet for a time and turn one's attention within is a great advantage in ordinary life, and this is one aspect of zazen. People these days have their heads boiling with thoughts and are ever turned outwards as if searching for something. They have forgotten how to still the heart and turn within for the inward vision. They know how to take a step forward, but not how to withdraw a step.

At the cross-roads there are lights, Go and Stop, to control the traffic. If there were only the Go and not the Stop, accidents would be inevitable. The Stop is essential. Modern people only strive to rush on, as if they were all in a horse-race, and they have lost the power of withdrawing and reflecting. They go ahead and go ahead, but in the end there is a deadlock, a real traffic jam, and they finish as pathetic victims of spiritual disaster. By paying attention to how to withdraw, by turning within and reflecting, one can reach the inexhaustible treasure there, can experience directly the Amitabha Buddha in the heart and the Pure Land paradise in the body.

In daily life when anger rises, when we are at the end of our patience, if before the outward explosion we restrain ourselves and turn within to reflect for five minutes, almost always relief will be found. A man once told me: "I am naturally quick-tempered, which was a disadvantage to me and a nuisance to others. But now when I get angry and resentment pours through me, I do not express it but shut my mouth and at once go before an image of the Buddha. I join my palms and sit five minutes in meditation. My family have taken to the idea also, and now we do not have quarrels. To have heard of the method of meditation has been a wonderful thing in my life." If we really mean to do it, we can always find the five minutes for sitting quiet even in the midst of affairs. It is no exaggeration to say that by this five minutes' margin almost all of the problems of daily life, great and small, can be solved. And if meditation is done deeply, the accumulated sins are destroyed and we can avoid creating new ones.

As to sins, there are those who complacently feel that after all they have never done any great wrong in their lives. Thus to feel that there have been no sins, to be unconscious of the sins, not to be fearful of committing sins—this in itself is a great sin. In Mahayana Buddhism, even if I myself be supposed to be without sin, yet while there is any sinner anywhere I must feel repentance for his sin. But when I reflect in silence, I inevitably realize how terrible and frightful are the sins of deed, word, and thought that I have been committing unknowingly from time immemorial. It is easy to refrain from murder or from theft in the physical sense, but are we not always committing those sins spiritually? It is no rare thing today for a man's life to be wrecked by others through the power of tongue or pen. Then there are the negative sins, cases where one could easily help and yet does nothing. There is a verse:

> In the evening,
> If it were rain we should seek shelter,
> But thinking: "It is only mist,"
> We go on and become drenched.

So we go on thinking it is nothing and all unknowing pile up great sins. Unless there is repentance for sins, they cannot be extinguished by making material amends. The only way to destroy them altogether is heartfelt repentance. Not to fear committing sins is itself a terrible thing. Again, to be frightened at one's sins, to shrink away from them and (as they think today) to escape from all one's sins by suicide —this is most regrettable and is one kind of sin.

9 (opposite). KABUKI DANCER.
"The stillness in stillness is not the real stillness . . ." (See page 132.) The dancer is Miss Ichikawa Suiho. A single strand of hair is deliberately left loose, illustrating an important principle of Zen.

10. THE KOAN OF JUDO.

". . . only when there is stillness in movement can the universal rhythm appear." (See page 132.) The *tori* (man executing the throw) is Mr. Matsumoto Yuzo.

To the Second Patriarch Eka came a man who said: "The body of this disciple before you has been caught by disease: I beg Your Reverence to absolve me from my sins. Now in dire straits from illness, I pray you to destroy my sins for me." Eka replied: "Bring the sins here, and I will resolve them." After some time the man said: "I look for them but cannot find them," and the teacher declared: "Then I have resolved them for you. Now live in accordance with the Buddha, the Law, and holy community."

The man said: "From my visit to Your Holiness I have come to know of the holy ones, but what are the Buddha and the Law?"

"This heart is the Buddha; this heart is the Law; the Law and the Buddha are not two."

"That there is no sinful nature either within or without or in the middle—this I have learnt today," the man said in gratitude, and the *Dentoroku* history tells us that from that moment the illness suddenly abated.

The inquirer must have been a man of elevated wisdom and character who had already practised the discipline for some time, and from this story we can see how in such a case the Zen training annihilates sins. It is said that by the virtue of a single session the sins are destroyed. If one's thought comes really into an awakened state, then just as the dawn bell smashes the dream, Sansara and Nirvana both become like last night's dream. The shadow of endlessly piled up sins vanishes, and not only that, but

> *The moon which rests reflected in the water of the pure heart,*
> *When the wave breaks, becomes light!*

Piled up sins are destroyed, and all becomes purified. In the chapter on non-duality in the Vimalakirti Sutra, a Bodhisattva explains sin and happiness from the point of view of enlightenment: "Sin which is the result of passions, and happiness which is the fruit of virtue, are imagined as quite opposed to each other. But seen in the light of true wisdom, each of them is no more than the activity of the Absolute, and we cannot speak of bondage or liberation." If in a sitting of meditation that true wisdom can be realized, sin and happiness both are only ideas we have been dreaming.

One sometimes hears that to practise meditation it is necessary to retire to a mountain away from society, or perhaps to bury oneself in some old temple, to discard humanity and become a so-called hermit. Of course, it may be that for the final training in seeing one's nature and attaining realization it would in some cases be necessary for a time, but this is not the object. Zen means to bring that power by which the Zen meditation is gripped directly to bear upon our present daily life, to vivify it. Withdrawing into meditation, and then advancing and handling affairs —this advancing and withdrawing, movement and rest, together, must be Zen. A master says that going about is Zen, and sitting still also is Zen. The Taoist classic *Saikondan* says: "The stillness in stillness is not the real stillness; only when there is stillness in movement can the spiritual rhythm appear which pervades heaven and earth." *(Plates 9 and 10)* An ancient adds: "Meditation in activity is a hundred, a thousand, a million times superior to meditation in repose." So greatly does he esteem meditation in activity.

The sutra teaches that by the practice of meditation the lake of the heart becomes pure and calm, and when the lake of the ordinary man's heart becomes pure, the reflection that appears within it is of a Bodhisattva. When the wellspring of the heart is purified, the wrong paths which otherwise appear as a result of his wrong actions, to that man become as if non-existent. How should there be wrong paths for him? The Pure Land is not far. As the phrase goes, "This heart becomes the meditation room." The world of light, of virtue, appears, and now our daily life has a changed meaning. In fact, for the first time our ordinary life becomes radiant with real meaning.

All Japanese know of the great painter Kano Tanyu,

whose work exists even today at the Myoshinji temple. This is the story of the time when he painted the great dragon on the ceiling of the main hall of the temple. It was his masterpiece and is one of the art treasures of the world. At that time the master at Myoshinji was the celebrated Zen master Gudo, famous as the teacher of the emperor. He had heard that the dragons painted by Tanyu were so realistic that when a ceiling on which one had been painted fell down by chance, some said it had been caused by the movement of the dragon's tail. When the painting of the dragon at Myoshinji was mooted, Gudo went to the painter's house and told him: "For this special occasion I particularly want to have the painting of the dragon done from life." Naturally the painter was taken aback, and saying: "This is most unexpected. As a matter of fact, I am ashamed to say that I have never seen a living dragon," would have refused the commission. The Zen teacher, however, agreed that it would be unreasonable to expect a painting of a living dragon from an artist who had never seen one, but told him to try to have a look at one as soon as he could. The painter asked wonderingly: "Where can one see a living dragon? Where do they dwell?" "Oh, that's nothing. At my place there are any number. Come and see them and paint one." Tanyu joyfully went with the teacher and when they arrived, at once asked: "Well, here I am to see the dragons. Where are they?" The teacher, letting his gaze go round the room, replied: "Plenty of them here; can't you see them? What a pity!" The painter felt overcome with regret, and in the event spent the next two years with Gudo, practising Zen assiduously.

One day something happened, and he rushed excitedly to the teacher, saying: "By your grace I have today seen the form of a live dragon!" "Oh, have you? Good. But tell me, what did his roar sound like?" At this query the painter was again at a loss, and for one further year laboured on at his spiritual practices. What he painted at the end of

the year was the dragon of Myoshinji, a supreme masterpiece in the history of art, remarkable for its technique but
far more for the life which the artist has infused into it.
It seems as if it contains the great Life which embraces
heaven and earth, the universe and man also. It was to pierce
through to this reality that the master painter Tanyu poured
out his heart's blood for three years. But when the one
experience of reality was attained, there was no need to
seek any further.

To hear a story like this is indeed wonderful, but attainment is no easy thing, and we must not allow ourselves to
be discouraged. The experience of reality transcends time.
The sutra says: "Heroes become Buddhas with one thought,
but the lazy people are given the three collections of scriptures to traverse."

CHAPTER SEVEN

When in reverence this truth is heard even once,
He who praises it and gladly embraces it has merit without
end.

THE SONG OF MEDITATION

THESE lines are still concerned with the virtue of the practice of zazen, but here, in particular, the merit of Hearing the Law. In the writings of Zen master Sho-ichi it is said: "This truth is the path to supreme liberation, and when once it has entered a man's ear, he is a candidate for Bodhisattvahood." The Mahayana is being spoken of, but the merit of Hearing the Law may be taken to apply to all the Law of the Buddha. In general, hearing the preaching of the Law is a most noble thing, and from ancient times it has been laid down that to acquire peace one must first hear the Law. There is a poem by one of exalted rank:

We should pass through flames to hear the Law—
What to say of rain, wind, or snow?

So he himself set out, disregarding the morning snow and the evening hurricane, to hear.

This *hearing* is one of the triad—hearing, thinking, practising—of which it is taught; by hearing, thinking, and practising we enter Samadhi. Samadhi is the heart of the way to enlightenment. *Hearing* means by the ear; *thinking* means pondering in the heart; and *practising* means the putting into actual practice.

Hearing with the ear, thinking in the heart, practising with
the body,
Soon sounds the bell of entry into enlightenment,

so runs an ancient song of the Way, and it is indeed so. It is important that we listen to this great Law, receive it deeply into our hearts, and so far as our circumstances allow, exert ourselves to practise it. In hearing the preaching of the Law the most important thing is faith. The scripture says: "By faith, know; by practice, prove." Through faith the Law first enters, then it is pondered in the heart, and then practised by the body—this is the order in which enlightenment is attained.

Certainly there are those who say that a little hearing or preaching of the Law is of little account. But these are people who are well advanced on the Way, and have forgotten how it was that they entered upon it. Today they have left behind the stage of the mouth and the stage of the ear; they are at the stage of practice, and reject hearing and speaking. Still, when a man is asked, for instance, to subscribe for some lecture meeting, even though he wriggles out of it, he has to listen to quite a lot about it. And in whatever way it may be, as the first step in entering on the path, hearing is important. But we are warned that there are three kinds of hearing. The first is what might be called shot-gun hearing: that is, to receive something from one side and shoot it out on the other side, retaining nothing at all. The second kind is like a basket: when something is put in, the real substance leaks away, and just a residue remains. The third kind of hearing is like digestion: getting rid of the rubbish and absorbing only the substance. In listening to the Law we must take care to hear in the third way. If not, the bliss is only second-hand; the ear is in paradise, but the ear alone.

When this blessed truth comes to the ear, namely when as a result of past good actions one is enabled to hear it, then he who understands his good fortune and reveres the Law, his blessedness is boundless and his merit limitless. In Buddhism, reverence for the Law is a special virtue, and what is most wanted in daily life these days is reverence.

We sympathize with others when misfortune or calamity overtakes them. That is truly a beautiful thing. At the time of the great earthquake in Japan it was indeed moving how the whole world extended its sympathy. Among individuals too, when an acquaintance suffers a mishap, sometimes we are surprised how fellow-feeling bubbles up in us. But where it is a case of good fortune, for instance if someone goes up in the world, how is it then? With our speech we congratulate them and tell them how glad we are, but as to whether we are really pleased about it, there is an old verse which gets to the root of the matter:

Good friends, but lately become distant—
This gentleman next door has built a new warehouse!

When the new warehouse is built, it is a sign of prosperity, and the neighbour pretends to be pleased for his friend, but really it is otherwise. Friends for a long time, but lately somehow they have become cold and distant. Pondering how it began, he realizes the cause is that "this gentleman next door has built a warehouse!" Isn't it mean? Isn't it narrow-minded? This is envy, the picture of a narrow and hateful human heart. Again, when we are confronted with virtue, with someone's good action, it is not just that we cannot rejoice in it. Probably it is to cover up our own absence of good actions, but it is not unusual not merely to fail to rejoice over it, but instead to sneak round to put a spoke in the wheel, and by hook or crook do some harm. How hateful and sinful! We are warned in the sutras that there are many terrible sins in this world, but there is none so terrible as to be envious of wisdom and virtue, and to spoil another's good action. Whereas there is no sin so terrible as envy of wisdom and goodness and spoiling a virtuous action, conversely it is needless to say what a noble and great virtue it is to revere from the heart another's virtue. It is rather easy to sympathize with misfortune or calamity, but it takes a good deal of a man to be able to rejoice at another's good luck or virtue.

It is not by chance that in the Buddhist code the virtue of rejoicing at the welfare of others surpasses even giving. Truly a noble thing, sublime and meritorious, the virtue of rejoicing for others. Now up jumps someone enthusiastically: "I agree, rejoicing for others is a fine thing. What you have said is right, and from now on I shall go in for it. Instead of striving for merit by giving money or breaking my bones helping those public movements or charitable activities which are such a nuisance, I shall watch the others doing it and afterwards rejoice and tell them how well they have done and how praiseworthy it all is! How fortunate that rejoicing rates higher than giving! What a wonderful religion Buddhism is!" This is the greatest of errors. He who can rejoice from his heart at the good deeds of another could never be satisfied unless he himself were performing them also.

The Song is referring to praise and rejoicing in connection with hearing the Law, but the real virtue is to feel them from the heart at all right actions. And the sin is not just a question of not doing right actions oneself, but being envious of them in others and wanting to spoil them, ending up as a mere tool of the passions arising from narrow selfishness, a mere slave to name and profit. The illustrious Emperor Kiso of the T'ang Dynasty in China once made a visit to the Kinzanji temple on the Yangtze River. At the temple the scenery is exceptionally fine, and the throne was set at the top of the temple tower, giving the best view of the river. The emperor was conducted to his seat. He saw on the great river countless boats, some going up and some going down, some to the right and some to the left, so that it might almost have been mistaken for the sea. He was overjoyed to see the prosperity of the country he ruled: trade and commerce thus flourishing—what we should call today a fully developed country. At his side was standing the abbot of the temple, Zen master Obaku, and the emperor remarked to him: "How many flying sails on the river,

I wonder?" In other words, how many ships would there be on the water. The abbot smoothed his robe and replied respectfully: "Only two." The emperor's satisfied expression was wiped off his face. What did he mean, with his two ships? Even now in front of one's very eyes were there not at least a hundred, perhaps two hundred? Two ships indeed! Was he making light of his emperor, laughing at him and making a fool of him? His face showed that the reply was not pardoned. "How two ships?" he asked. Zen master Obaku's expression showed not the slightest disturbance. Respectfully he answered: "Here are only the ship of name and the ship of profit." Name means seeking for reputation, and profit means seeking for gain. As Your Majesty sees, there are many ships on the river, but one half of them are sailing for fame, and the other half to make money. The ship of name and the ship of profit, only these two are on the river. Pondering the thought, the emperor gave a deep, deep sigh. It was as the abbot had said. In administration, in economic strength, in industry, in education, the culture of the T'ang dynasty can only be called brilliant. But what of the people who participated in that culture? If their motive was not name, it was money; if not money, then name. Apart from these two they cared for nothing. Then like thunder from a clear sky the emperor gave sweeping orders for reform. In that moment he saw the truth, and from his determined policy arose the famous culture of the great T'angs.

The parallel is not far to seek: is not the condition of Japan today like that? There is unprecedented prosperity, and it must be called a brilliant civilization. But of the people, there are hardly any who are not wrapped up in money or fame. Those who have obtained them are regarded as well off and fortunate, and are flushed with pride, and those who haven't them are disappointed and discouraged, writhing with hatred of everyone and curses on the world. Isn't it so? This philosophy of name and money is an all-important problem; ugly and narrow as it is, people make it supreme in their lives and depend entirely on those two things for their support. But we have to think of our real nature and get a right understanding. We must not lose the Way here. If we are lost in these things, the rejoicing at hearing the Law will hardly arise and paradise will be far away.

In whatever age, the problem of name and money has always been the worst. It is on this point that we go astray or are enlightened, that we sink or swim. There are only two alternatives: to be a king who can use name and money, or to be a slave rushing about in pursuit of them. Many people are entirely the latter. There is the following story: In a certain zoo, a famous tiger died. The owner of the zoo was worried about the effect on the popularity of the place, and finally formed a plan to have the skin taken off and get someone to go inside to play the tiger. It was not easy to find a man, but finally a drunken good-for-nothing took the job for a salary of thirty yen a day plus three quarts of the rice wine called sakè. Every day this man used to don the tiger skin and go into the cage, where he attracted the gaze of the public by posturing lazily in front of them, from time to time having a drink of the sakè he had with him in the skin. One public holiday the zoo was crowded. There was a tremendous mass of people in front of the cages of the tiger and his next-door neighbour, a lion. Among them were two merry students. One of them said: "There's no animal so strong as a tiger. You know that old poem all about the tiger's roar and the towering mountain and the moon above—well, it's right. Look what a terrific one this is. . . ." The other retorted: "Nonsense! The lion's the king of the beasts, and when *he* roars all the others tremble. Everyone knows that. And just look at this lion here, what a beauty he is!" From this a quarrel developed, which ended in their asking the owner of the zoo to pit the two beasts against each other, he to be indemnified for whatever loss he might incur. Hearing this, the "tiger" was terrified, but before he could do anything the lock on the door to the next cage was opened, and the lion bounded furiously in. The crowd held its breath. Shaking, the tiger got to its feet. For a little while the lion seemed to play with the other like a cat with a mouse, and in so doing its mouth came against the tiger's ear. A voice came: "You needn't shake like that—I'm a three-quart man too!"

There is more here than just a satire on modern life. All modern people do wear a skin, it is true. But from the standpoint of Hakuin's teaching that all living beings are from the very beginning Buddhas, this humorous tale has a special meaning. Lions and tigers, in different forms, they are pathetically posing before the spectators as exhibits in a show. But in them is living always a noble human being. There are only two alternatives: to live hidden by the skin, or to throw it off and live openly.

> As the mind of its possessor
> It becomes a treasure or an enemy—
> The yellow gold.

The metal itself has no value; the thing is whether one is able to use it or not. There is a Western saying that money is the best of servants and the worst of masters. There is nothing noble in money; the nobility is in being able to use it. It isn't difficult to get rich; the difficulty is to find the right Way. Hakuin tells us:

> Until he is confronted by wealth, who knows the inner heart of the virtuous man?
> Until he is confronted by difficulty, who knows the loyalty of the retainer?

Certainly most people these days prefer doughnuts to flowers.

> What sort of cherry-viewing party is it without a drink?
> What sort of husband is it without money?

Fuddled by dreams, they pass between tears and laughter. It is in the face of money that the Way is most difficult.

> Desires on the heart, and snowflakes on the ground;
> As they pile up, the Way is lost.

> Weeping,
> But with a keen eye for their share
> Of the dead mother's possessions.

The latter poem, by Abbot Ikkyu, describes with brutal frankness the selfishness over money.

> Don't worry over it; deposit your money with the world.
> The rascals who want it, let them work for it.

And if they get it with their sweat and elbow-grease and honest effort it is alright. But today it is just the reverse. People do not want to get it in the proper way by their sweat and toil. They think themselves hard done by unless they can get rich in some interesting, amusing, and pleasant way. An old woman put up a notice for certain of the customers in her wineshop:

> You buy on credit and the accounts pile up and it's bad business.
> Come with ready money, and I will gladly serve you.

A customer quietly replaced this with another which read:

> Buying on credit, I feel I am getting it free.
> When I have ready money, I go elsewhere.

Nothing to choose between them. What is needed today is to reflect on ourselves. The world is like a tub of water. When we want water, we keep scooping it to us and to us, and it comes rushing, but at once goes past and away round to the other side. On the other hand, if we push it away and away and away to the other side, it rushes away from us but at once is coming round to us again. So we are always trying to get money for ourselves, always for ourselves, but we do not get very much. As we get it we are losing it. But when we begin thinking for others and are doing everything for them, we lose everything, but in fact we are gaining it. The ideal is to see that our own interest is that of others; if we make our own interest the objective, we do not make a profit, and if we make the interest of others the objective, we do not take a loss. Gain in this world is like the water swirling round in the tub. When we realize in practice that our own interest is the interest of others, and can praise and rejoice in the Zen meditation of the Mahayana, for the first time we are freed from the wrong paths, and paradise can manifest itself.

■ CHAPTER EIGHT

How much more he who turns within
And confirms directly his own nature,
That his own nature is no-nature—
Such has transcended vain words.

THE SONG OF MEDITATION

THESE four phrases make clear the confirmatory experience of one's own nature, which is the aim of Zen meditation. The phrase "turn within" means turning the light so that it shines back. If the light of self-consciousness is turned and shone back onto the nature of one's own mind, then can be perceived one's absolute nature; the self-nature suddenly becomes something absolute—it is in fact no-nature. Even the word "no-nature" is not really right. The distinction of nature and no-nature is at an end; discussion of self-nature and other-nature is extinguished. This is the stage of actual experience, truth transcending the stage of discussion and absolutely beyond vain words. All words have become mere prattling and nonsense talk. Hearing about the great truth of the meditation of the Mahayana, praising it and rejoicing in it—even that brings wide and great merit. How much more to turn within and confirm directly one's own nature, namely to turn the light and shine it back into one's very self, to experience what one's own nature is! This is not mere listening but tasting directly; nay, not mere tasting but grasping it oneself; not explanation that all beings are from the very beginning Buddhas but knowing from direct experience how they are from the very beginning Buddhas. It is entering the realm of experience, knowing for oneself that self-nature is no-nature.

When we understand that there is no ice apart from water, or in other words, that water and ice are not two things but one thing, then we do not need to make the distinction that *this* is water and *that* is ice. It is as if it has all become water. Similarly, while we stick to distinctions and cannot see their sameness and non-duality, there are Buddhas and there are demons, but once we confirm by experience what our self-nature is, there is no hell and there is no paradise. It has all become absolutely the same. This is called the real awakening. When we awaken to this state of absolute Sameness, we still see distinctions between mountains and rivers, grass and trees, the earth and men and beasts, but for the first time we do not stick to the distinctions we see. We have in ourselves the great experience of infinite freedom, that the distinctions themselves are Sameness, and the Sameness is the distinctions.

We can understand the method of turning within with the help of a passage from Zen master Daikaku: "Turning round his light which lights all the outer things, he focusses it within on the inner self. Mind is bright like the sun and moon; their light is unlimited and infinite, and illumines all regions within and without. Where light does not reach is dark, and such is the demon-cave of the Black Mountain. There live all demons. The demons harm man greatly. It is like this with mind also. The wisdom-light of mind, unlimited and infinite, illumines all states within and without. Where it does not reach is dark. We call it the shadow-world of ignorance. There live all passions. The passions harm men greatly. Wisdom is bright: the illusory ideas are shadow. Light illumines things. Turning the light so that it shines back means not letting the light of our thought wander here and there, but directing it at our own original nature. This is also called universal illumination, which means the state where error and enlightenment are still unmanifested. People today think that the illusory ideas are their essential mind, and want to reach happiness through their passions. When should they ever get free from the cycle of birth and death?" These wise words are worthy of our special attention. As to the state attained by turning the light back, once reached, it is not a question of analogies about ice and water or other explanations, but like knowing for oneself whether a thing is hot or cold. It is the gate of real experience, transcending the gate of discussion, and quite beyond vain words. Academic study is only talk; religion is real experience. One who understands religion theoretically is merely a sort of professor of theology. Now just as a professor of economics is not necessarily able to become rich, so the man who by taking his stand on intellect alone hopes to have the religious experience is like one hoping to get water by digging in sand. Religion must aim at actual experience for oneself. If not, then like the blind men who investigated the elephant, we shall learn no more than a single surface or corner of the outer skin of life and the universe.

Long ago there was a king named Mirror-bright. He invited a number of blind men to examine an elephant. They were afterwards to tell him about the form of the elephant. The blind men stretched out their hands and felt the elephant to ascertain its shape. The one who touched its foot reported that it was like a tree. Then the one who felt the tip of its tail said that the elephant was like a bamboo broom. The one who touched the tail itself said it was like a stick. He who touched the belly said: "The elephant is like a great drum," while another who touched the trunk said it was like a great snake. He who handled the ear said it was like a winnowing-basket, while the man who felt its side said: "Like a wall," and the one who touched the tusk said: "Like a great horn." Each, being sure it was as he said, wrangled endlessly with the others. "Blind, are they not blind?" marvelled the great king, "Yet they stick to their views as if they had sight." The story is told in the Classic of the Six Perfections.

In this way all they said was just a kind of vain talk. It is no more than an illustration, but the man who has not found what his own nature is, who has no light of knowledge, is the same as a blind man. Those today who judge religion by everyday experience, or discuss faith under the light of science and philosophy, are in a way blind men examining an elephant. They get some idea of one surface or one edge, but it cannot be said they are close to the real truth. And their world is not the reality of confirming directly their own nature, that their own nature is no-nature, transcending vain words. We have to enter the region of the absolute Sameness, where one's own nature is no-nature, and confirm the meaning of becoming Buddha in this very body.

We are always opening our mouths and howling for the realization of some ideal. But when that ideal is realized, then what? To put it in religious terms, we trudge along one of the traditional paths and make progress by our practices, some of us dreaming of heaven and others praying to be reborn in some paradise. Neither of these things is bad. But the question is: having got up to heaven or arrived in paradise, what after all do we do then? There is a story about an old lady who every day used to take her little grandson to pray at a Buddhist altar. One day the boy noticed the candlesticks on the altar, which were in the form of a crane and a tortoise. He opened his eyes very wide and asked: "Granny, why are the crane and the tortoise there?" The grandmother replied: "Well you know, the crane is supposed to live for a thousand years and the tortoise for ten thousand, and they're very lucky creatures, and here they are on the beautiful Buddha altar, like the Pure Land paradise." The little boy asked: "When the crane's thousand years are over, what happens to him then? And the tortoise, when his ten thousand years are gone, what happens to *him?*" She said: "What big questions for such a little boy! Surely you know that. After a thousand years, the crane dies, and the tortoise after ten thousand years dies." The grandson opened his eyes wide again and asked: "After they die where do they go?" The old lady was getting out of her depth, but she couldn't admit she didn't know, so she said: "I'll tell you. The crane and the tortoise are lucky creatures, and the moment they die they go to the Pure Land." Her grandson's eyes were like saucers as he asked: "Granny, when the crane and the tortoise go to the Pure Land, what happens then?" The old grandmother was now in deeper than ever, but she said firmly: "This little boy doesn't know anything, it seems. Why, when they go to the Pure Land, they turn into candlesticks!" The boy innocently swallowed it and subsided. Nevertheless, his question was a penetrating one, and how is it to be answered? The question remains for us. Certainly it seems alright to say that when the crane and tortoise go to the Pure Land they become candlesticks, but after they become candlesticks, then what? And then what? It is not just the problem of the crane and tortoise. When we ourselves go to the Pure Land, then what? Are we to stand in rows there for ever, like dolls ranged on the shelves of the Pure Land? Do we just sit on the flowers of the lotus-lake there, rocked by the breeze? In short—then what? There is an old popular song:

> Your whining "Then what? And then what?"
> The more you ask, the stupider you get.

But the fact is that we have got to penetrate to the ultimate, beyond all words. The Chinese verse says:

> By travelling, at last you will come to the end of the stream;
> By sitting patiently, finally you can see a cloud forming.

What happens in the end? Unless we inquire: "Then what, then what?" in our coming and going, and finally rest in the ultimate, lasting peace will be hard to find. Our hopes are always like wanting to climb up a hundred-foot pole.

When we have climbed it we have the problem: then what?

Kusunoki Masashigè, after his last great battle at Minato-gawa when all his resources were spent, was going to turn his sword on himself, but on an impulse rushed with his sword still bloody to Zen master Soshun at the nearby Kogonji temple, where he used to attend in times of peace, and asked: "At the meeting of life and death, what then?" Now the last moment has come. This instant when life and death meet, how am I to meet it? To which Master Soshun replied: "Cut off both the heads; the one sword gleams cold against the sky!" O Masashigè, you are a monster with two heads, life and death, sprouting from your shoulders. With that sword you bear, quickly cut off both the heads of living and dying. Then that single brilliant sword will be glittering in the heavens. Masashigè could not grasp the meaning, and asked again: "What is the end of it all?" and the Zen master gave a shout: "Katsu!"* The hero broke into a sweat from head to toe as the realization came to him, and galloped back to the battlefield. The story is well known how after the last furious fight he and his younger brother, vowing to return to serve the loyalist cause for seven more lives, serenely ended their lives here and entered life eternal.

This great cry of "Katsu!" in answer to the "and then what?" is from the state transcending words. It is from the realm of realizing one's own nature. Sho-ichi in one of his Zen sermons speaks of the living communication beyond words and phrases. "The sacred syllables of the scriptures are not mere letters, but the true mind of all living beings. For the sake of the one who has lost his true mind they present various similes and words so that the true mind may be realized and the delusion of birth-and-death may cease. But the one who awakens to the true mind, who returns

* This is a shout traditionally used to give the pupil's mind a shake.

to the source of his being, is able to read the real scripture. The words are not the real sutra. If we maintain that mere verbal recitation is all, well, are we able to keep warm in the cold weather by saying 'fire' or to keep cool in the heat by saying 'breeze'? By shouting the word 'food' can we satisfy our hunger and be filled? In fact, we do not get warm by calling 'fire!' or find water in our mouth by saying the word. These words and phrases are like things in a painting. You can call your whole life long, but your hunger will not cease. Alas, the ordinary man is sunk in the delusions of life and death, and from the things of the world is ever eagerly hoping to get something. But it is the height of folly." So he explains that the only way is direct realization of one's nature.

In the sayings of an ancient master there is this: "The Way is not attained by mindfulness *(yushin)*, nor will it be attained by mindlessness *(mushin)*; it is not reached by purity and silence, and to be even a fraction involved in verbal concepts is to be a thousand, a million miles away." Again it is said: "Zen is not words and phrases. Nor is there an exclusive creed to give people. Under this doctrine you cannot insert even a hair. It is direct grasping. The Buddhas of the three worlds draw in their tongues; the great patriarchs gulp back their words." This is the real turning of the light within and directly experiencing one's own nature. Zen master Muso has a verse on the Buddha's sermon-without-a-sermon, and Kashyapa's hearing-without-hearing:

The words which explain all without explaining—
Few are the ones who can hear them without hearing.

It is well known how the devout Emperor Go-mizuno-o always used to go to hear the Law from master Gudo at the Myoshinji temple. The room and the seat he used are now preserved as national treasures at the Shoso-in repository. There is a poem by this emperor which expresses the single essence of all things from the standpoint of direct realization:

Everything heard with the ear or seen with the eye
Is that One, and not apart from the Law.

In these times you might say that we have reached a deadlock in everything. Deadlock in politics, deadlock in economics, in knowledge, in education, deadlock too in morals, virtue, and religion. The so-called slump is not just in our economy, but there is a slump appearing everywhere in our life. As a result of the deadlock we seem to be driven by restlessness, a kind of feverish frustration. How is the deadlock to be broken? How can we be rid of our fever and unrest? We have reached a point where modern man, with all his vain boastings of the marvels of science and his admiration of materialistic culture, has to stop and think. No amount of whining self-pity will avail. What matters is the present: what are we to do? Many people these days, however urgent a question may be, put it aside and think: "Well, let's get on with earning our living." There is a verse by someone:

When hunger and cold are set against love,
I blush to say it, but hunger comes first.

True, one cannot set aside the stomach; its cry is keen and worthy of our sympathy. We must practise material benevolence and mutual help. But the great mistake is to think that by providing bread and jobs all our problems can be cleared up. The basic problem is that our present culture, concentrating solely on the conventional and material side and ignoring the mental and spiritual side, ends in tying ourselves in knots, and even in suicide. As a first step in the matter, let me ask: When you get your food and jobs, what then?

A normal man, when his character and intelligence are rightly and naturally developed, can never get satisfaction unless he attains spiritual conviction. Take as an example the control of our actions. When small children stand naked, we tell them: "If you stand naked like that, the Thunder Man will come down and steal away your little tummy-button." Then they snatch up their clothes and put them on. If they want to run out at night, we tell them about the goblins, and they get frightened and don't go out. Though this sort of thing is of course only superstition, it does control the actions of little children. When they go to their first school, these things will not work. There aren't such things as goblins, and they do not believe in a Thunder Man. But when they are scolded by the schoolmaster for something, that has a big effect on them. Then they come to middle school and lose their fear of the teacher. He is only an employee of the school, and if the students go on strike they can perhaps get rid of him, they feel. Still, though they are no longer afraid of the teacher, they know that a wrong action is against morality. They know that man's duty is to act righteously, and they are guided by morality and ethics. Going on, they become high school or university students, and are dissatisfied until they have examined what we mean by the words "good" and "bad," and the scientific and philosophic reasons why we should follow ethics and be controlled by morality. One more step and they question whether there is any scientific and philosophic reason at all; they cannot find satisfaction in ethics and become sceptical and critical of any ideal. Now they get worried and distressed and can easily lose all peace of mind.

When in this way we have gradually advanced from the instinctive to the superstitious, to the common-sense, the scientific, and to the philosophical, we must go on to transcend all these stages and stand finally in reverence before the unseen, in awe before the unheard. But since the Meiji Restoration towards the end of the last century, our culture has become estranged from this vital religious teaching. We feel today an inner unrest, and this, as it were, searching after something is really the religious desire. Clearly there are many defects in our culture. What is essential, whether in universal questions or personal questions, is to understand the spiritual secret of returning to the essence of the soul. We must press the inquiry "and then what?" right to the end, penetrate the ultimate, and then for the first time we can get the right answer.

We human beings cannot be satisfied with the instinctive world, with the world of superstition or the world of common sense, nor can we rest in science or philosophy. We have to reach the world of conviction and reality. We must not be caught in the world of so-called name and fame, nor think that the world of learning is all, but must enter directly the world of freedom, the world of things as they really are. We must sport in the world of direct realization of our true nature. This is the world of truth transcending vain words, where words have been left behind, where, as it is said, the self-nature is no-nature. This is the ideal world, where all doubts whatsoever are resolved. Where shall we look for it? We must wait in the realization that self-nature is no-nature.

◼ CHAPTER NINE

> *The gate opens, and cause and effect are one;*
> *Straight runs the way—not two, not three.*

THE SONG OF MEDITATION

THESE two lines are a direct expression of Zen enlightenment, the peace that comes from realization that cause and effect are one. The ancients spoke of a universal net from which nothing escapes, and indeed there is nothing in the world so rigid as the law of cause and effect, or karma. If there is a cause, an effect is inevitable; where there is an effect, there must also be a cause. The proverb says that seeds which are not sown don't sprout, and you don't get eggplant from a melon vine. The Buddha teaches in the sutra: "If you wish to know the past, then look at the present which is the result of it. If you wish to know the future, then look at the present which is the cause of it." In the Kegon Sutra it is said that in each and every thing karma is clear to see.

When in this way distinguishing cause and effect, when speaking in the ordinary way about karma from the point of view of distinctions, Buddhism has the doctrine of the Six Causes, Four Associations, and Five Effects. The most important thing to note is that besides cause and effect, Buddhism also teaches association. With three principles: cause, association, and effect, the notion of karma is made more complete. From the same shoots, the blossoms will differ according to how they are manured and looked after. In this example the shoots would be the cause, the manuring and tending the association, and the blossoms the effect.

154 ◼ A FIRST ZEN READER

Generally association is included under cause, and so we speak of karma as cause-and-effect. Normally when we distinguish cause and effect we think of it vertically, as a question of time, just that they come at different times. But from the Zen point of view they can be viewed on the same level, under the light of Emptiness, of Sameness. They are seen as the same, without distinctions. In the Zen view absolutely everything has its root in mind, and all the phenomena are manifested by mind; when seen in this way, everything in the world has in fact a temporary illusory existence only; it is a momentary appearance. On this illusory temporary existence is imposed the pattern of cause-and-effect, but in fact cause and effect are one and the same. When the Zen Samadhi is practised, the universality of the truth-body is experienced and the oneness of cause and effect; the way is not two, not three, just one. The eye opens which can see cause and effect as the same. From the very beginning this oneness of cause and effect, namely the world of enlightenment, has been there, but with the ordinary eyes one cannot ever see it, and of course it is beyond the sphere of either science or philosophy. The phrase in the text, "Straight runs the way—not two, not three," comes from the Lotus Sutra: "There is only one way, not two nor yet three." The sutra extols the one peerless way of the Lotus, and the Buddha here teaches the one path as the final doctrine. Here "one" is not used in the mathematical sense as opposed to "two" or "three"; it is just that there is no "two," no "three"—cause and effect are all one Sameness.

When the wind blows hard on the sea, the waves rise, but once the wind drops, where are the waves? The body of water becomes the waves, and the body of the waves is only water. Cause and effect may be separated by a long time, but they are not divided into two. When cause is effect and effect is cause, when cause and effect are all one Sameness, it is proof that enlightenment is attained. It is the world of satori. It sounds as if cause and effect are negated or disappear, but that is not so. In principle, the three states of time exist as last year, this year, and next year; as yesterday, today, and tomorrow; or in an hour, in a minute, in a second—down to the tiniest fraction of time. What happens today is the result of yesterday and the cause of tomorrow. Here is a seed which is the result of last year's flowering and the cause of next year's flowering. The one thing is at the same time cause and effect. One man is at the same time a son and a father. Parent and child are distinguished according to the relation of cause and effect. Most people would smile if asked which came first, parent or child, but it could be argued that before anyone could be a parent he would have to have been a child; therefore the child must be the cause and the parent the effect. So in theory also we can see the oneness of cause and effect.

The oneness of cause and effect is not a mere theory, but something actually experienced. Cause is effect: effect is cause; they are not two! When we can know that enlightenment and delusion are one, when we experience the non-difference of cause and effect, then to our sight there is nothing obscure and to our action nothing impossible. Straight runs the way, not two, not three; no obscuring of cause-and-effect and no being obscured by cause-and-effect —truly, infinite freedom is clear before us.

No longer controlled and caught by cause-and-effect, not now a slave to it, instead of fearing it a man goes with it and can use it. They say that when the law is known it is feared, but the one who penetrates to the truth of cause and effect, to whom they are one, begins to worship the profundity and beauty of the law. The more we realize the great truth that karma is in all the worlds, the more we realize how unswerving it is, the more we are filled with reverence. The gate opens, and now we see the absolute, all-pervading, and undeviating nature of karma. In ordering our daily life, there is nothing better than a realization of the law of karma. In the No play *Aoi-no-ue* (Lady Aoi), by Zeami Motokiyo, the ghost of Princess Rokujo sings: "In this world transient as a flash of lightning, there is none to hate, nor need any pity me. Oh, when did I first become a ghost? Did I not know that the kindness done is not for the sake of the others, and if I suffer harm from another, surely I shall be recompensed?"

If we look at society today we can see how few people have an understanding of the law of karma. If good infallibly produced good, and evil always was followed by evil, then the law would be admitted by all. But how about it when we see the opposite happening? Everyone knows of bad people who do only bad actions, and yet are they not prosperous, do not things go well for them? And are there not good people, always engaged in righteous actions, who have nothing but bad luck? Is it not a matter of chance, after all? These facts are bound to give one pause. To resolve the question, first we have to think what we mean by good and bad luck. What people normally call good luck may not be so at all. Even where it brings a temporary happiness, how long is it before the happiness changes to sorrow? If we look at the working of karma in the infinity of worlds, we find it never wavers: good produces good, evil produces evil. We see an evil-doer flourish for an hour and ask ourselves whether wrong-doing is not, after all, bringing him a good result. But the water always flows downwards. Though when we see a mountain stream striking a rock and leaping up, we might say to ourselves: "Well, is not the water going upwards!" it is only for a moment, and in the end it falls down and down and never stops till it reaches the sea.

People who doubt the law of karma always say that the facts do not support it and that it is not justified by experience. The old verse says about this:

Speak not about ice and frost to the insect which lives but a summer day,

Nor tell of the ocean to the frog in the well.

Insects like the fireflies, born in the hot summer morning and dying in the evening, will not believe if they are told about how the snow falls and the water hardens into ice in winter. The frog born in the well, growing up there and dying there, will not listen to stories about the distant ocean. Their actual experience does not justify such beliefs, does it? They cannot accept them because that would not be in accord with experience. And this attitude is not unreasonable. Their experience, the facts before them, do not justify such beliefs. So one should not speak of winter to the summer insects, or of the ocean to the frog in the well, but only pity their ignorance.

It may be suspected that the modern ignorance of the law of karma, especially in regard to its role in daily conduct, is like this. The old verse says:

> *The artisans cannot make a fire-chariot like those of hell,*
> *Yet I have constructed this self, and I ride in it.*

Cause-and-effect is all-pervading; one acts oneself and reaps the results oneself, tying oneself and binding oneself. There is no escape from it. As in the line from *Aoi-no-ue,* "If I suffer harm from another, surely I shall be recompensed," we must understand that the changes of circumstance are all governed by karma. Zen master Sengai, warning against egoity as the great human failing, says:

> *"As to that, now I. . . ."*
> *Yes, but put not the emphasis on self—*
> *Emphasize the others, O emphatic man!*

People like to talk emphatically: "If it were *I*. . . ." "Now *I* should. . . ." Instead let them try asking: "If it were *you,* how would *you*. . . ?" When there is this spirit, things will go well in the family and in society. Sengai teaches the secret of serenity in life:

> *When I regard them as good and myself as bad,*
> *My very faults become virtues in their eyes.*

But when, as nowadays, people take themselves as the standard and must have it that they are in the right,

> *Because I am regarding myself as good and them as bad,*
> *My very virtues become hateful to them!*

And life becomes a series of clashes.

The scripture says that the world is the shadow of our own mind, and before railing at our shadow for being bent, let us correct ourselves. Takuan has a poem:

> *Good and bad are not in them but in my own self;*
> *When the form is straight, the shadow will not be crooked.*

The Sutra of the Layman tells us: "If you are reviled, contain yourself in patience; if you are praised, humble yourself inwardly. When treading the way, do not feel proud. When you see divisions, make peace between them. Reveal the good points of others and conceal their weakness; do not proclaim the shame of others." These are the important things in daily life.

The peak of spiritual living must be a life of gratitude, going with the law of karma. It means satisfaction with the past, gratitude for the present, and spiritual energy for the future. Past and future here do not necessarily refer to past or future births. As to the past, of course we must not fail to learn from our failures or forget to repay a debt of kindness. But in general, past is past; there is no point in grieving, and we should stop going over it again and again in our mind. We should accept the law of karma as right, and be content, not complaining about whether our present condition is deserved or not, but feeling gratitude. It seems rather negative, but there is happiness in living content with the circumstances. Here are one or two old poems:

> *If we look up, this way or that, everywhere it is star-*
> *spangled.*
> *If we only look down, there will never be stars.*
>
> *Rain is well and wind too is well, when we realize*
> *That in this life there is nothing completely good.*

> *The mountain stream will at the very end become the sea;*
> *For a time it passes beneath the fallen leaves.*

Each of the three verses is in its own way instructive.

When people are told they ought to live in gratitude as a part of spiritual life, they assent so long as things are going favourably, but when things keep going against them, they complain that it is unreasonable to expect them to feel grateful. But of course a man who has material prosperity, a healthy body, and who gets what he wants, feels grateful. That is natural, and it does not need any spirituality or discipline. The real spirituality is to live in gratitude when circumstances and things go against us. The nun Rengetsu when on pilgrimage came to a village at sunset and begged for lodging for the night, but the villagers slammed their doors. She had to make a cherry tree in the fields her shelter. At midnight she awoke and saw, as it were in the spring night sky, the fully opened cherry blossoms laughing to the misty moon. Overcome with the beauty, she got up and made a reverence in the direction of the village:

> *Through their kindness in refusing me lodging,*
> *I found myself beneath the blossoms on the night of the misty*
> *moon.*

As human beings we cannot avoid sorrow and hostility sometimes. But if we can change our thinking and feel gratitude, these things become blessings and increase our faith. When we can be satisfied with the past and rejoice in the present, then we get the spiritual energy to labour for others, as a return for blessings received. Spiritual effort becomes natural. This is the life of satisfaction in the three worlds; in other words, living contented with what happens.

> *When we realize that everything in the world has its limits,*
> *Then there is contentment in the humblest cottage.*

The same thought, that all is limited, teaches us the spiritual courage for the battles of life, as in the verse of Kumazawa Banzan:

Let misfortunes pile up even more,
And I will test the limits of my strength against them.

As to the future, we are to go in serenity and a spirit of gratitude:

We do not know, this autumn, what rain and storm may come—
The task for today is to weed the rice field.

He who can live like this is in the Pure Land paradise already. Good luck and ill luck, prosperity and misfortune—after all the mind is one only. As it is said, there is still grief even in the imperial palace; there is yet happiness with no bed but the earth.

Once Lord Yasushina, head of the Aizu clan, asked the teacher Yamazaki Ansai what had been his blessings in life, and he replied: "There have been three. First to have been born as a man, and second to have been born among educated people where I could learn to read the sacred books." As to the third, he paused but then went on bluntly: "The third, which is the greatest, is that I was born in poverty and not as a noble." The lord thought this strange and asking further was told that to be born in a noble household meant to be brought up by women, to have one's opinions flattered by servile retainers, and to end up as a fool. The lord smoothed his robe and looked down.

Vimalakirti, in the sutra named after him, speaks of the ideal life in metaphors taken from the family. "Wisdom is the mother; action is the father. The mother gives birth to the light-child; the father brings him up. All the Bodhisattvas are born of these two parents. With rejoicing in the Law as the wife, sincerity the son, compassion the daughter, and worldly passions as the servants, the six perfections of giving, good conduct, endurance, energy, meditation, and prajna as friends, he lives in the house of inner serenity. In the garden of the Absolute the trees of the holy doctrine produce the blossoms of satori and the fruit of enlightenment. The lake of liberation is unbroken by waves, and the water of meditation is pure; the fragrance of the lotus of the Buddha heart reaches afar. With relatives and friends, all rejoice in the holy hymns. . . ." and so on.

We should make our daily life in this way. Teachers and spiritual leaders in particular cannot lead others without themselves awakening to the truth of the oneness of cause and effect and acquiring enlightenment and spiritual energy. Everyone talks about this as the age of civilization, and this thing or that thing is hailed as a triumph of civilization. But in fact, civilization and education and religion are all a matter of the mind of the people. Real civilization means seeing rightly, hearing rightly, and thinking rightly.

It is not a question of waiting first till we understand all about the Noble Eightfold Path, and then hoping righteousness will develop; the fact is that an impulse towards righteousness is already a manifestation of the Noble Eightfold Path. All human beings have the capacity for seeing, hearing, and thinking aright. All beings are from the very beginning Buddhas, and truth and sincerity are a manifestation of their Buddha nature. The truth and sincerity which pervade the whole universe, when manifesting in humanity, appear as reverence for gods and Budhhas, as universal compassion, and in daily life as faith. Goethe divides respect into four: in relation to superiors, in relation to equals, in relation to inferiors, and in relation to self—in other words, self-respect. He bases his system of education on these four. Goethe further says that faith is the consummation of knowledge, not the beginning. Kant says that honour is a word used only in relation to human beings. But from the spiritual standpoint it can have a meaning in relation to the supernatural as well as the natural. In the Lotus Sutra the example is given of the Bodhisattva who saw the Buddha nature everywhere, and so in whatever direction he faced he used to join his palms and worship.

Saint Gyokai sings:

> *I pick up and cherish as jewels in my sleeve*
> *The stones and tiles thrown at me.*

Reverence brings illumination into human life; love brings blessings; and faith brings power. Reverence, love, and faith—these three become real morality and afterwards manifest as real spirituality. From that alone can a real civilization arise. Education today is in a most tragic state because the connection with religion is not understood. We pray the gate may open and the oneness of cause and effect be realized, and straight may run the path, not two, not three. Then the world will manifest as light.

■ CHAPTER TEN

Taking as form the form of no-form,
Going or returning, he is ever at home.
Taking as thought the thought of no-thought,
Singing and dancing, all is the voice of truth.

THE SONG OF MEDITATION

LIKE THE previous lines, these describe the state of realization. It is perhaps comparatively easy to reach the state where cause and effect are one; the realization of the universe as Sameness comes from that knowledge which is fundamental to man from the beginning. But the important thing is to go on from there, and through the other knowledge, which manifests after satori, we are to see the differences of form once more, and undertake the salvation of all. It is not simply a question of having satori and waking up from a dream. The aim is to wake up and then be active. This is a specially important point which is frequently misunderstood. If Zen is practised to get realization for one's own release from the sufferings of birth and death and right and wrong, it is not the Zen of Mahayana. The aim must be to take a jump beyond realization, or in the Zen phrase, to take one step more from the top of the hundred-foot pole, and return to this world to extend the hand of compassion to all that lives. Traditionally, great stress has always been laid on the practice undertaken *after* satori, the so-called maturing in the holy womb. In this sense, the upward-looking path is rather the means of Zen, and the downward-returning path is the goal.

There is the same idea in the Pure Land sect. Higher than

those who sacrifice their accumulated merit that others may attain the Pure Land are the ones who, having attained the Pure Land, return to human birth to bring others there.

Many people in the world suppose the purpose of life is simply to be successful and make a name for themselves, but it is a great error. What to do after that, after achieving success and fame? The problem is to find the ultimate goal of human life. To those who are wholly devoted to success, and still more to those who are about to achieve it, who are on the crest of the wave, I would say this: "If this success is the goal of life, then consider how afterwards you will have to endure the grief of the inevitable decline."

> *Be not too proud!*
> *For the fullness of the moon*
> *Is but a single night.*

We should lay it to heart. The goal of human life is not what the world calls success. If we use the strength and virtue that give worldly success for a goal transcending the world, we can attain immortality. The purpose of life can be fulfilled only in this way.

The essence of the supreme liberation of the Zen path and training is the Samadhi of sport. After the gate opens and cause and effect are one, they take as form the form of no-form, and going or returning there is nowhere not their home. First the distinctions of illusion are left for the Sameness of realization, but then in that Sameness, if a man falls into not seeing cause and effect at all, the Sameness itself ends by becoming an illusion. Food and dung are the same to him; he becomes a Zen demon who swallows up heaven and earth. But if he continues in the practice of seeking the original face, there is no danger of falling into the wrong Sameness, and he can take a further step, from Sameness to the distinctions again. As the text says, he takes the form which is no-form as form.

In the non-duality chapter of the Vimalakirti Sutra, a Bodhisattva named True-sighted explains form and no-form from the highest point of view. Some think that the statements, "all things are one form" and "all things are of no form," are entirely opposed, but in fact all phenomena, having no determined self-nature, are born and die in accordance with karma-associations and so are fundamentally the void. They are without form and also with form. With a form, because without form; without form because with a form—in this way he explains the doctrine of no-form and no-limitation.

The text speaks of the form of no-form. Generally in Buddhism the word "form" means all forms, everything that is perceived, and we are warned that these are temporary manifestations of an illusory character. They are all classified under the four: origination, continuance, change, and destruction, or in popular language, birth, age, illness, and death. The world and the things in it first originate, then continue for a certain time, then change, and finally perish. So everything passes through the four states between its beginning and end. As to human beings, first they are born, then they become older, then fall ill, then die, so passing through birth, age, illness, and death. These states are called "form." This is all from the standpoint of distinctions, and when the state of realization is entered, we come to see them as Sameness, in other words the true "no-form." Here the form is no-form. But if we cling to that very no-form, inevitably it becomes just as much an illusory view as the form. For a realized man to cling to his satori is like a kind of illusion. There is one more step to take, so that the form again appears out of the no-form; the form is no-form, and the no-form is the form. It is not a satori of absolute Sameness. By the practice of Zen meditation we can go from form into no-form, and then from no-form into form. The supreme satori is that the state of no-form, where all is the void and one Sameness, should be at the same time the state of distinct forms where there are mountains and there are rivers, and yet that we should not be deluded by the distinctions. The lines, "In that not-a-single-thing is an inexhaustible treasure; there are blossoms, there is the moon, there are towers," refer to the form of no-form.

In this state the stream in the valley is His great tongue, the colours of the mountain are His pure body, as Sotoba says in his poem. When he realizes that going or coming he is ever at home, then there is no hell to fear or paradise to gain. The mountains, rivers, grass, trees, the whole earth as it is, are the radiant Pure Land. Tears and smiles both are manifestations of the voice of truth. That peace of the heart cannot be spoken; it is the state of heaven itself.

Having grasped the phrase about the form of no-form, we can understand in the same way what he means by the thought of no-thought. Thought here means all our delusive discriminating; in other words, wrong thinking. When wrong thinking is abandoned there is right mindfulness (shonen), which is the technical word for the sixth of the eight steps of Buddha's eightfold path. Right mindfulness or right thought (shonen) is pure without any distraction, and so it is also called no-thought (munen). From this no-thought we must again enter thought, but now free from illusion People think that munen or no-thought is to be like a dead tree, entirely without mental activity, but it is quite wrong. Munen or no-thought never means to become a mere stone, but it means to stay in shonen, right thought or right mindfulness. In that shonen when the thoughts of distinctions arise, "in spring, the flowers; in autumn, the moon, in summer, the breeze; in winter, the snow; if in the serenity of the heart there is no attachment, all seasons are well." It is freedom and bliss; singing and dancing all are the voice of truth. It is the Samadhi of yugè or sport. The word means literally to sport or play, and the sense is that just as in play we do as we will, without forcing the mind, so this Samadhi is spontaneous action for the liberation of all.

There are people who do a little practice (and in particular dabble in Zen) and before attaining any spiritual light jump up without thinking at all and come out with pointless big words and fine phrases. They go in for every kind of oddity to show how different they are and think carelessness and unreliability are spiritual freedom. Wit they pass off as enlightenment and frivolity as detachment; they specialize in speaking and acting as if mad. This company of clowns cannot be mentioned in the same breath with the spiritually enlightened who "take for thought the thought of no-thought."

Long ago in China, to Zen Abbot Kosen came a man, a dabbler in Zen, to show off his attainments. Punning on the abbot's name, which can mean "flour," he asked: "Is it wheat flour or rice flour?" The abbot unconcernedly replied: "Try and see." The man lifted up his voice in a roar in imitation of the shout employed by some Zen masters, but the master only said: "Haven't you a cough, haven't you a cough!" and patted him on the back. There are many half-baked ones of this kind today also.

Master Rinzai tells us that spiritual power means to be able to enter the world of forms yet not be subjected to the delusion of forms, and so with scents and tastes and the rest; when one knows they are all empty, they cannot bind him. Again he explains that such a one entering fire is not burned, entering water is not wetted, and if he enters hell it is like sporting in a garden. For him, singing and dancing is all the voice of truth; standing or sitting he is always in conformity with the right—that is the spiritual state of the truly enlightened.

> The water-bird in its path leaves no track
> Yet it never forgets the way.

Such is the Samadhi of sport, or the Samadhi of spiritual manifestation. All lives that can be called really holy are of this kind: perfectly harmonious, free from all restrictions, and yet lives of selfless action overflowing with compassion.

A great example is the life of Hakuin, who in his eighty-four years dominated the spiritual world. With his speech and writing, he "entered the city with open hands" in the Samadhi of sport. A master of the school which does not take its stand on letters, he was yet rich in words, and his literary production was immense, particularly in the field of the popularization of Zen. Of course he left many technical works, sermons, poems, and hymns, but at the same time he taught the Way by means of popular songs, by everyday conversation, by writings in the colloquial language, by working songs, songs of the Way, and "wild songs." Among the writings in the popular language is the Song of Meditation itself, a masterpiece famous then and now. His pictures were innumerable, many of them strange by ordinary standards and not a few flouting convention, but today they are preserved as treasures in many families. In training disciples he was supreme, and they flocked to him from all quarters. Round his grave at Shoinji temple are the graves of disciples who happened to fall ill and die before completing their training; there are scores of them. Among many spiritual lights produced by him, Abbot Zuio and Abbot Torei can be called his two holy pillars. Both attained the Samadhi of sport and illumined life—going or coming, they were yet ever at home.

Through his pictures and writings we can glimpse Hakuin's spiritual sport and freedom. Tokutomi Soho says of them: "Abbot Hakuin's pictures of Bodhidharma are self-portraits. The Chinese characters of his calligraphy, sometimes like old ropes, sometimes wormlike scrawls, sometimes like knots of bracken, are pictures of the mind. Though the forms are so different, without exception they reflect something of the abbot himself. From the productions of his brush the abbot can be known, and again no one who does not know the abbot can fully appreciate his pictures and writings." These are penetrating remarks.

Hakuin drew a picture of a beggar, and on it wrote a

poem: "Whoever it may be, if when young he is a wastrel, squanders his money, and finally is disloyal to his parents, then that young master ends like me, with his stomach empty and racked with hunger. Can you spare a copper?" Surely to the tramps of today such a poem will be bitter to hear.

On a picture of the fishermen who go out with cormorants at night with a fire to attract the fish:

The fire of the cormorant fishers is truly
The fire of hell before you. Beware! Beware!

On a picture of the magic hammer of the god Daikoku, which grants prosperity:

The hammer strikes and endless treasures appear—it is a
lie!
This is the hammer to smash the arrogance of wealth.

He painted a picture of Hotei, a god of fortune, holding out one hand and saying: "O young people! Whatever you say, unless you hear the sound of one hand you are only skinfuls of nothing!" Whatever you learn, whatever you know, while you cannot hear the soundless sound of heaven and earth, it is all meaningless. A poem in praise of the round Daruma (Bodhidharma) doll, which is weighted so that however much it is rolled over it always comes upright at last:

Giving up good and bad,
He comes upright in the end,
The little priest!

On a picture of Abbot Ikkyu holding a skull:

This—is anyone;
Beware, beware!

On a picture of Hotei and another of the gods of fortune ladling out rice wine:

Happiness! To sit leaning
Against the pillar
With congenial friends,
And hear the clink of cups!

What a human feeling there is in this poem! A man wrote a verse questioning whether there is a next world or not, and Hakuin replied with another verse:

Does the next world exist or not?
'Tis indeed a maze.
None knows but the asker himself. Go and seek him!

(You have lived before, and this is the life after death.) Who else is to decide the question? This is his counter-question. A poem on the pangs of separation:

Even at the first meeting there is already the future separation.

Would there were one to stay with us always like a shadow!

What is there, he asks, which we can have with us for ever and never lose? The poem to a tea-ladle is this:

It passes through the cold hells and the burning hells,
But it has no mind and does not suffer,
The tea ladle!

This is the great Zen meditation: "when the mind functioning ceases, fire itself is cool." To the woman disciple O-san he sent a drawing of a *hossu* whisk *(see Plate 4)* and a broom, with the Chinese poem:

The three sages and their tiger asleep together,
And snoring like thunder!
When hearing it, understanding dawns,
Kanzan and Jittoku come again.

(Kanzan and Jittoku are two of the three famous wild sages referred to.) To this she replied:

The broom to sweep away the thorns of worldly wrong thinking—
Who can compare with Hakuin of Harajuku!

There are some children's riddles entitled "The Village Headman's House, Its Fortune and Lineage":

What is like the honest carpenter's work?
The village headman. Why?
Because he whittles away the mura. *(Mura means "unevenness" but also "village.")*

And what is like a ripe fruit deep in the mountains?
That headman's house. Why?
Because it perishes altogether and is lost in oblivion.

If people took the song to heart, the prosperity of their line would be assured. It does not apply only to that old village headman.

On his picture of the god Daikoku (god of fortune, whose name also means "black") he wrote:

His stature is short,
His colour is black,
But how touching his smiling face!

True it is. There is a picture of the mice in meditation round a human teacher, and on it:

The teacher of the mice one day held up a mallet and preached
  his sermon:
"Let any cat's head come, and I will strike the cat's head!"

By Hakuin's creative inspiration the Zen master becomes a teacher of mice, and the coming of enlightenment is changed to the cat's head. Again he has a picture of mice wrestling and on it written:

In the breast of each of us
Are two mice, one black and one white.
The white one is of white deeds and right mind,
The black of black deeds and evil thoughts.
Black and white are always struggling
Like a pair of wrestlers.
If the white wins—oh noble!
All adversity is converted into fortune;
The right actions, the ten virtues, are all his;
The three bodies and four wisdoms [of the Buddha] *are*
  assured.
If the black wins—oh base!
All luck is converted into bane;
The seeds of prajna-wisdom are chewed and destroyed;
The holy fruit of bodhi is consumed utterly.
From but one wrong thought,

> We incur immeasurable and endless sufferings.
> Not only in this life the harm,
> But in long future lives we suffer dumbly.
> As ghosts, as brutes, ox and horse, we shall suffer,
> Our life dragging on through the lower worlds.
> The god of fortune, though his name is Black,
> Yet hates the black. Take heed, O people!

On a picture of Bodhidharma:

> Journeying in Chinese Gi and Ryo,
> You transmitted the Seal of the Heart;
> Sporting in Japanese Kai and Shinano,
> I have reviled your Zen.
> The doctrine you brought from the West
> Has been scattered like dust;
> Your spiritual children of the Eastern Sea
> Are dissolved as salt in water.

Hakuin brushed the Chinese character "death" on a hanging scroll, and to it wrote a poem:

> O young people, if death is hateful, die now!
> Dying this once, you will never die again.
> The sorrow and bitterness of this world will become happiness.
> You are called samurai. Should you not be ready to die?
> Despite brave words, the samurai who has not died this once,
> When the crisis comes will flee away or hide.
> The feudal lord gives you silk clothes and white rice
> So that he can rely on you in that hour.
> Even a blade by a master swordsmith, if the samurai does not realize he has it,
> Is of as little use as if girded on a midwife.
> He who has once died in the depths of the navel—
> The spear of the master spearman cannot touch him.
> He who dying while yet alive carries out his duties—
> The arrow of the master archer is nothing to him.
> The samurai who has passed away deep in the navel circle

Finds no enemy in all the world.
Throw away all, die and see—
   The god of death and his demons stand bewildered.
In the field of the elixir at the navel, meditate on the Lord
   of the mind and see—
   At once all is perfection, living paradise.
Though one know how to rest firm in virtue,
   If he cannot meditate, he has not yet attained.
Meditation is the inmost secret of the knightly way;
   While yet you live, practise meditation.
Do not meditate only hidden in a dark corner,
   But meditate always, standing, sitting, moving, and resting.
When your meditation continues throughout waking and
   sleeping,
   Wherever you are is heaven itself.
After practising thirty or forty years
   We can know that we have meditated a little.
Though one boast: "I have died," if he shows selfishness
   he is yet unenlightened;
   Loyalty to superiors, love and reverence to parents.
Though one boast: "I am enlightened," if he is heartless
   to living beings,
   He falls to the demon world—so says the holy word of
   Kasuga.

We have looked at one aspect of the Samadhi of sport;
its taste is something to be savoured in tranquillity. We have
seen how the blissful sport is itself great teaching and enlightenment. We too should perform our daily duties in
the Samadhi of sport, in bliss and fearlessness, and then our
life will be a direct help to society and to the country.

■ CHAPTER ELEVEN

Wide is the heaven of boundless Samadhi,
Radiant the full moon of the fourfold wisdom.

THE SONG OF MEDITATION

THESE two lines express enlightenment and the perfection of the fourfold wisdom. There is the phrase "boundless Samadhi." The word Samadhi is Sanskrit, and can be translated as "right thought," and sometimes as "evenness," the meaning being a state where the mind is one and undisturbed, with no distracting thought. Boundless *(mugè)* means without restraint, unobstructed by anything, absolute freedom. These lines read on from the previous lines about the form of no-form and the thought of no-thought. On the surface of a mirror, good and bad, right and wrong, for and against, absolutely all worlds are seen as the same. So it is said that all objects are reflected in the self and the self again is reflected in all objects, like two mirrors facing each other with nothing between. The heaven of freedom of boundless Samadhi extends below and above and on all sides, and in it the full moon of the fourfold wisdom is radiant in its splendour. The four wisdoms are these: the wisdom of the mirror, the wisdom of Sameness, the wisdom of spiritual vision, and the wisdom of making perfect. The mirror-wisdom is that into which the eighth or "store" consciousness, in which are latent the seeds of taints and passions, is transformed; the wisdom of Sameness is the transformation of the seventh consciousness or thought-centre; the wisdom of spiritual vision is the transformation of the sixth consciousness or sense-centre; and the wisdom of making perfect is the transformation of the fivefold sense-consciousness. (The classical Buddhist psychology makes this division into eight consciousnesses.)

To state the doctrine very briefly: in the mirror-wisdom, as in a great mirror, shine all objects, perfect and without defect. Then by the wisdom of Sameness the differentiation of self and others, of this and that, is abandoned and they are seen as the same; the distinctions are left, and the Sameness is realized. Supreme compassion is born from this vision of universal Sameness. The wisdom of spiritual vision sees all rightly and with love, in themselves and in relation to each other; a treasury of all good qualities, this wisdom enlightens living beings and ends their delusion. The fourth wisdom is that by which is done all that has to be done and which brings it to perfection; for the welfare of all it performs actions and shows itself variously as the Buddha's body of manifestation.

The four wisdoms are the fruit of Buddhahood and through them manifests fully the Buddha's action. As the great Mirror which illumines all, there is nowhere he does not reach; seeing all clearly in the light of Sameness, he has no partiality; his spiritual vision is never deceived; and then out of his great compassion he brings to perfection all the candidates to perfection The manifestation of the three bodies of the Buddha is the application of the fourfold wisdom. The dharma body has to do with truth; the bliss-body, with wisdom; and the body of manifestation, with action. The Five States of the Soto sect, the Four of the Rinzai, are also only the practical application of the fourfold wisdom.

It might be supposed that the wisdom, or the three bodies, are for Buddhas alone, but it is not so. Zen master Rinzai says: "If you desire not to be separated from the Buddhas and patriarchs, then just cease looking outside. When the thought in your mind is the light of purity, that is the truth-body in you. When the thought in your mind is the light of non-discriminating, that is the bliss-body in you. When the thought in your mind is the light of not making differences, that is the body of manifestation within you. Those three bodies are you who are now before me listening." What a delightfully direct sermon, to be sure!

The state attained by Zen meditation, where by the power of the boundless Samadhi the fourfold wisdom and the three bodies of the Buddha appear, is spoken of as heaven and the moon. Wide is the sky of Samadhi and radiant the moon of the fourfold wisdom—the doctrine is expressed in poetic terms. Needless to say it does not refer merely to some distant Buddha-world; we must never forget that the real reference is to what is close, our own mind. Hakuin always teaches from the standpoint, "all beings are from the very beginning Buddhas." Talk about Zen training must not be mere idle spinning of a web of words, but must relate to our practical spiritual advancement. If it do not, it is doubtful whether any real peace will be attained. In brief, we should see through to the essence of the mind, should bring out the spiritual light of the mind to the full, and the spiritual action of the mind without restriction. The world which then appears is not the world as now seen by our little wisdom and limited vision, but is perfect and without restriction, namely without "I" and without body. That world without the limited I is the ultimate ideal. An ancient sings:

Throw away the little mind which is called the I, and see:
There is no limitation in all the three thousand worlds.
Of my home the blue is the ceiling and the earth the carpet,
Sun and moon the lamps, and the wind the broom.

The heaven of Samadhi and the moon of wisdom must be manifest in daily life. Here is a verse of a great one of the past:

There is no place where the moon's beams do not reach,
But it is in the heart of the beholder that their brightness dwells.

It is the heart of the beholder that is important. Not-I means the Great I, and the actualization of the world of not-I must be the supreme ideal of humanity. The whole life of Zen master Hakuin was this alone.

There is a well-known story about him when he was at Shoinji temple. A girl among the congregation became pregnant. Her severe father bullied her for the name of the lover, and in the end, thinking that if she said so she might escape punishment, she told him: "It is Zen master Hakuin." The father said no more, but when the time came and the child was born he at once took it to him and threw the baby down. "It seems that this is your child." And he piled on every insult and sneer at the disgrace of the affair. The Zen master only said: "Oh, is that so?" and took the baby up into his arms. Thereafter during rainy days and stormy nights he would go out to beg milk from the neighbouring houses. Wherever he went he took the baby, wrapped in the sleeve of his ragged robe. Now he who had been regarded as a living Buddha, worshipped as a Shakyamuni, had fallen indeed. Many of the disciples who had flocked to him turned against him and left. The master still said not a word. Meantime the mother found she could not bear the agony of separation from her child, and further began to be afraid of the consequences in the next life of what she had done. She confessed the name of the real father of the child. Her own father, rigid in his conception of virtue, became almost mad with fear. He rushed to Hakuin and prostrated himself, begging over and over again for forgiveness. The Zen master this time too said only: "Oh, is that so?" and gave him the child. As soon as the truth became known to the world, the master's spiritual fame became a hundred times what it had been before.

This story has been the subject of a play and also of various songs. But how would it be if such a thing happened to us? Some people will object: "Well, that was in the old days, but it couldn't be done now. If one took that

line nowadays, one would become an orphanage. . . ."
Others will profess deep sympathy and admiration. Helping others, and at the same time making a name for oneself! They would like to imitate the Zen master; perhaps they have even got the ragged robe in readiness. But then, they reflect, in these days the authorities would never permit a child to be thrown out like that. And so after all, the sympathy and ragged robe are not needed.

The real point of the story is the Zen master's great spirit of non-egoity. We should try to fathom the spirit of this attitude. In our life we are too narrow, too much imprisoned in our ideas of I and mine. Are we not always impelled by love and hate, afflicting and tormenting ourselves? We should try how the moon of the fourfold wisdom will dispel the black clouds of selfish delusion, so that we are no longer lost in the world of right way and wrong way.

In the No play called *Semimaru*, the sister of Semimaru is a madwoman who wanders about with her tangled hair standing on end, and singing a song of right and wrong. "The third child of the imperial house am I, who am called Hair-on-end. I was born a princess—on account of what karma is this? In my mind wild confusion, a madwoman of remote places and border lands, my green hair grows climbing towards heaven. Though I brush, it will not keep down." Singing, she shakes her hair, and as she raves the children follow her laughing and mocking. She turns, and becoming calm for a moment, reproves them: "Why do they laugh, the children? Is it that my hair is funny, growing the wrong way? Truly things the wrong way are funny, but more than my hair, their laughing at me is the wrong way." Again she sings: "Strange, strange, the world before the eyes of the people! Seeds buried in the earth rise up as the twigs of a thousand forests; the moon riding in heaven is reflected sunk in the depths of the myriad waters. All see these things as right, but I call them upside down. I am a princess, yet I have descended among the common people;

my hair growing upward is bathed with the star dew. How they call one thing the right way and another the wrong way—strange it is!" So sings the madwoman, and indeed it is strange. We should end our agony in the maze of right way and wrong way, and see through clearly. We are happy when things go right for us and resentful when they go wrong, now laughing and now crying. But to understand what is really right and what is really wrong, we must see through to the truth of right and wrong. When we do so and give up our little wisdom and narrow vision and clinging to delusions, we shall not be caught by any condition but can shine through them all and act freely with unshakable conviction.

The wind blows, but the moon in heaven is not moved;
The snow piles up but cannot break the rock-sheltered pine.
With unshakable conviction, right vision and right mindfulness appear naturally. The Shrimaladevi Sutra says: "When there is faith in the words of the Buddha, the conceptions of eternity, bliss, self, and purity arise. Then there is no contrary thought, and this is called right vision. Why is this? Because the truth-body of the Buddha is the perfection of eternity, the perfection of bliss, the perfection of self, the perfection of purity, and awakening to the truth-body is what is called right vision." With right vision, the right mindfulness of the enlightened appears.

Another sutra says: "The Bodhisattva does not attend to other things, but just to the self. Why is this? Because awareness of his own mind is awareness of the mind of all. When he is free from cravings in his own mind, he is free from the cravings of all. When he is free from the anger in his own mind, he is free from the anger in all. When he is free from the foolishness in his own mind, he is free from the foolishness in all. In this sense he is called omniscient." Vimalakirti knew that there is no birth, age, sickness, or death, but for the sake of living beings he manifested an illness, to show that when there is illness in anyone it is in the Bodhisattva because of the unity and harmony between them.

In ancient times in China, Abbot Hojo asked the famous Baso: "What is the Buddha?" He replied at once: "The mind, the Buddha." Abbot Hojo had practised many years, but this seemed to knock away a block in his mind, and he immediately had a great realization. He went to Plum-tree Mountain, where he built a hermitage. Baso, hearing of this, sent a monk to ask him: "What did you obtain from the master that you have come here and live like this on the mountain?" Hojo replied: "He told me, 'The mind, the Buddha.' I attained it and now am living here on Plum-tree Mountain." The monk said: "Do you know that recently the master has changed the Buddhism he preaches?" The abbot asked: "How has he changed?" The monk said: "The master now teaches: no mind, no Buddha." Abbot Hojo shouted: "The old master! Still bewildering the people! But though he make it 'no mind, no Buddha,' still for me it is just 'the mind, the Buddha,'" he concluded quietly. The monk came back and told this to Baso, who commented: "The plums are ripe." Our conviction, our spiritual vision, should be like this.

The spiritual state of Samadhi and wisdom is reflected most clearly in daily life as indifference to life and death. Knowing the truth about them, he is free of both. Zen master Sengai painted a picture of his own passing away into Nirvana, like the famous pictures of the Buddha passing into Nirvana with all the mourners round weeping. Sengai made his picture deeply touched with daily life, for the rice plants and the radishes have come to join in the weeping. Dangling from the branch of a pine-tree is a straw bundle, and the poem of farewell:

What drops from the pine-branch?
Bean soup!

The meaning is that in the bundle is a jar of his favourite bean soup, which is also a purge. When Sengai's disciples asked him (on his deathbed) for the traditional last words, he wrote: "I don't want to die." Thinking this would not do, they asked him again, and this time he wrote: "Really I don't want to die." Not wanting to die, or hanging on to life, or limitless compassion—right is the unfeigned human feeling, and he does not permit speculation about anything else.

When coming, knowing whence coming;
When going, knowing whither going.
But when clinging tightly to the side of a cliff,
In the thick clouds he does not know where he is!

Dokuon, who was abbot of Shokokuji temple at the end of the last century, was asked by a guest for a death poem and said: "I will not write a death poem. Because I don't like dying." And he did not write one. It is interesting to compare this with Abbot Sengai.

A contemporary of Dokuon was Tekisui of Tenryuji temple, who left this death poem:

I no use to the world; the world no use to me.
The great universe a mustard seed; Mount Sumeru balanced
*   on the palm.*
Oh this follower of the Way! If not mad, then stupid.

Muso Kokushi expressed his realization, transcending birth and death, with this:

Since nothing has come into existence from anywhere,
Why grieve over its returning?

The loyal minister Fujifusa, with the fugitive Emperor Go-daigo on his back, came to Kasagi Mountain. Lord and subject, both starving, thought to shelter from the stormy night under a pine. But the dew fell from the tree, soaking the emperor's robe, and the minister, weeping at his master's plight, joined his palms and made a poem:

What can I do? I sought the shelter, but even here
Our sleeves are wet with the dew.

This noble and faithful minister later entered Myoshinji temple, and after many years of hard training meditating on Original Perfection, he had the great realization and ultimately became abbot. When in the world, he was a great minister labouring for his master and his country; then as a great Zen teacher he worked for the salvation of the whole world.

The activity of realization is no-activity; the work is no-work, it is only a manifestation of light. A poem by Master Dogen reads:

Never thinking of protecting the little rice fields,
Yet it does not fail—the scarecrow.

There is an old song:

Not for the sake of a beholder, in the deep mountains
Blossoms the cherry out of the sincerity of its heart.

The great activity is when the world and self become one, when all things and self are seen to have the same source. From that state of realization the light is again shone to where he stands. Then every movement of his hand, every step with his foot, spiritualizes what he meets; he makes spiritual use of every event and thing. Before and after his footfall, the breath of holiness is born.

The green of the willow is the graceful form of Kannon;
The wind in the pines is the sermon of salvation.

At the front gate the willow's green expresses the grace of the Bodhisattva Kannon; behind the temple the whisper of the pines is the voice of the sermon.

The old pine declares the prajna;
The silent bird revolves the absolute.

Truly the ancient pine is speaking the holy words of the mystic prajna scripture; the bird motionless on its branch holds the secret of the absolute. When flowers are red and willows green as they stand, this is the miraculous state, the manifestation of the spiritual absolute. Miraculous yet not miraculous, spiritual yet not spiritual—because when all is holy there is nothing specially to be called holy. It is the world as it is, the world of Thusness *(tathata)*. When the heaven of Samadhi opens wide, the truth and the way are

11. FUKUROKUJU, GOD OF GOOD FORTUNE AND LONGEVITY,
    BY OKA KYUGAKU.
"Good fortune deep like the sea;
Blessings piled up like a mountain." (See pages 186–87.)

before the eyes, are under the foot. To put it a little more directly, heaven and earth are in the self, everything is endowed with the self. The moon of the fourfold wisdom illumines all and leaves no dark corner. What is called realization, what is called illusion, is just having this or not having it. The sage, the ignorant, is only having and using it, or not.

The modern way with everything is to investigate by analysis and dissection, but instead they destroy the life of the thing. So while they talk of construction, what they do leads to destruction. In the essays of Hatosu he relates how a man of this sort peeled off the skins of a scallion one by one, and at the end found he had nothing left. "There is only skin; there is no real scallion at all," he concluded. This is worth remembering. Peeling off the skins, he was destroying the thing itself, and taking its life. If instead he had buried it in the earth there would have been something. There would have been life; sprouts would have come, and it would have flourished.

Zen master Rinzai says: "When he is ever the lord, at once all is Truth, and there is no slave. When he becomes the lord, everything around him comes to life. The living path to Buddhahood and liberation is to take the stand ever on the self, always and everywhere to be the lord and master, to concentrate on where one stands and bring to life what is before one."

To talk of Samadhi or wisdom while spinning Utopias or fantasies in a world of dreams, is to end as a sleep-walker. Zen always warns us to turn our light on the place where we stand. Saint Jiun used to say: "Satisfied with the day, and satisfied with the place where he is, the superior man acts and reveals his greatness." If each brings this great spirit and feeling to his task, in his own province, the environments will rectify themselves, and step by step prosperity will come. Every day is a good day; in every place the Pure Land reveals its glory; the Buddha light appears in the earth we stand on. *(Plate 11)* We shall be blessed with real success and lasting peace. Hakuin's whole life was shining the light onto the place where he stood. The fruit of it is the wide heaven of Samadhi and the glory of the radiant moon of wisdom.

■ CHAPTER TWELVE

*What remains to be sought? Nirvana is clear before him,
This very place the Lotus paradise, this very body the
Buddha.*

THE SONG OF MEDITATION

THESE lines expressing the peak of realization conclude the
Song of Meditation. After attaining the great freedom of
limitless Samadhi and the wisdom of Buddhahood, there is
nothing more to seek. Before Nirvana was revealed, while
the view of illusory distinctions was not abandoned, there
was the Buddha to seek and the passions to be repulsed.
But after realization, there is no bodhi to be sought and
no passions to be cut off. The three thousand universes become his own; he need not get out of Sansara; he need not
pray for bodhi. Rinzai in a sermon says: "So long as the
man intent on doing the practices still has any aims at all,
he becomes bound again by those aims, and in the end
cannot attain what is in fact easily attainable. In my own
view, there is nothing at all to be sought. Once seated above
the Buddhahood of the bliss-body and the body of manifestation, the completion of the Bodhisattva's ten stages is
only an imposture, and attainment of the rank of enlight-
enment-of-sameness or enlightenment-of-holiness is an iron
fetter. Those who long for such states cannot attain Buddhahood. As for the eminence of the *arhat* and Pratyeka
Buddha (who seek enlightenment for themselves alone), it
is like a dunghill." In such extreme language he expresses
his view. As the Song says, when Nirvana is revealed the
world is the Lotus Paradise, and when it is not revealed all

kinds of obstacles appear. He who seeks Buddha is caught by that Buddha and does not attain realization; he who seeks realization is caught by that realization and cannot attain Buddhahood. But if he is a true follower of the Way, by virtue of his Zen meditation Nirvana is revealed to him then and there. Now as the current takes him he wears out the old karma, putting on whatever garments come to him, when he is to go just going and when he is to sit just sitting, with never a thought in his mind of hope for Buddhahood or looking for anything. In the natural course, he is in Buddhahood. Indeed there is nothing so great as this taking of not-taking, nothing so noble as the seeking of not-seeking.

Long ago in China, Zen master Obaku, who had reached the highest peak of spiritual attainment, was yet seen constantly worshipping the Buddha with great devotion. Struck by a doubt, a disciple asked: "Are you asking something of the Buddha, or seeking something concerned with the Truth?"

The master replied: "I have nothing to ask of the Buddha or to seek about the Truth."

The disciple asked again: "Then why do you worship?"

The master said: "I simply worship."

Such is the high worship. To bow the head before another, the head in which there is a hidden motive, is nothing. Again, the bow when one meets an acquaintance has no meaning. But "simply to worship." It is seeing truth! The culmination of greatness is the action based on seeing truth. There is a poem by Gudo Kokushi:

> From the very beginning, the Buddha truth is nothing strange to us:
> Drinking tea, eating rice, and putting on clothes.

To the great one whose action is without seeking anything, going and staying, sitting and lying all become the Buddha truth, the Buddha activity, and the Buddha conduct. So an ancient says: "If he performs action in order to get the Buddha, the Buddha himself becomes the badge of this San-sara." The foolish Yajnadatta thought he had lost his head, it is said, when he turned away from the mirror and could no longer see it reflected. When the mind rests from its seeking, that is peace, that is the serenity of Nirvana. When the eye of realization is opened and there is real conviction, this very earth is the Lotus Paradise, this very body the Buddha, and there is no need to go anywhere else at all. Without moving a step towards a heaven beyond, he finds the Lotus Paradise, the heaven of the Pure Land, here and now. It is a world of light. The existence of the Pure Land paradise in the West is not thereby denied. The Pure Land is all-pervading and universal; it is here and it is there. With the revelation of Nirvana, the place where one is becomes the Pure Land, and the body the Buddha. The old song is interesting:

> *No paradise of the East, no paradise of the West—*
> *Seek along the way you have come. They are all within*
> *you.*

The Pure Land is not different from this body, and its Bud-dha is not other than this mind. When we attain what is called the Pure Land of consciousness only, the Amitabha Buddha of the self, we see the nature and become Buddha. Zen master Munan has in one of his sermons: "The great resolve to go into a mountain retreat is a noble aspiration. Do not fall away from it. But even if one does go far into the mountains, he is not outside the transient world, and if he still has his mind unchanged, what will it serve to change the residence?"

> *Outside of the mind there are no mountains*
> *Wherein to build your solitary hermitage.*

There are two old verses:

> *He escapes from the world into the mountains, but there too*
> *Sorrows still come, and now where is he to go?*

> *O plover birds, let not your minds be disturbed,*

For whatever beach you visit, there too the waves and wind
will rise.

Outside the mind there is no place to go. It is the mind itself that is the first object of our quest, and also the last.

Milton says that by the mind heaven is made into hell, and hell made into heaven. But the mind is a rogue, and we cannot be negligent. An old song of the Way tells us:

It is the mind itself which is bewildering the mind.
Do not set free the mind to the mind!

When Eka, the second Zen patriarch in China, was still in the stage of spiritual seeking with its attendant pain and suffering, he made a long journey to see the great teacher Bodhidharma. He was not granted admittance, and stayed several days outside in the snow. Finally he cut off one arm as proof of his sincerity, and with the blood running down cried: "I pray the teacher to pacify my mind for me."

Bodhidharma said: "Bring your mind here, and I will pacify it for you."

Eka said: "I seek it, but I cannot grasp it."

The teacher said: "Then I have pacified the mind for you." The other immediately had a realization and later was invested with the succession as Second Patriarch.

We must understand for ourselves the great truth contained in the phrase, "I cannot grasp it." Zen makes penetration into the mind its central principle, and to rest quiet on the mind its aim. The life of Zen attainment is not like standing on a river bank watching the current and appreciating the water or the landscape as a witness; it is jumping into the current and becoming one with it, but without being drowned in it. It is to ride the current and be united with it. There is a Zen verse:

On the swift current is impelled a ball,
Freely turning and turning, freely rolling and rolling.

When we are one with the current driving the ball, heaven and earth and self become one, and changing with them we help the evolution of the universe.

This is the main point of the Song of Meditation. It begins with the great premise that all beings are from the very beginning Buddhas. Then there is the winding course from the six paths of ignorance up to the peak of attainment; and finally there is nothing more to seek, for Nirvana is revealed; this very spot is the Lotus Paradise and this very body the Buddha. The language of the Song is simple, but the more we go into it the more profound and mystical are its depths. We must not stop at just thinking about the ideas of the Zen master, but must study them, practise them, and at last attain direct experience. The Zen taught by the master with such great energy in his life was an outstanding contribution to the spiritual culture of his country.

Always in history those who love fighting are destroyed, but those who are not able to fight are also destroyed. Virtue and strength together, such alone lasts and can lead others aright.

In our daily life we should remember three things: joining the palms as in prayer, bowing as in worship, and charity. Joining the palms is the best posture for bringing the body and mind into a state of unity; the bow means honour and respect for others; charity is the basis of peace in society. If we practise them, it is certain that we shall in turn receive.

Again there is a phrase most important for daily life: "For the ideal, seek the high; for the practice, honour the low." It is an old Zen saying: "His will treads the head of Vairochana; his practice is to prostrate himself at the feet of a child." It should be pondered deeply. The ideal must be as high and noble as possible, namely a consciousness which would set its shoe on the head of the truth-body of Vairochana Buddha. But the practice must honour the lowly; in practice he must bow his head at the feet of a running-nosed youngster. In humility he puts himself among the meanest.

What the Mahayana teaches is to destroy the wrong and

reveal the right. Virtue and power, being and non-being—the true middle way of the Mahayana does not incline to either side. Such must be the aim of our culture. In the world today (1934) is the propaganda of extreme internationalism, with the slogan of class warfare, leading to the error of Marxism, and on the other side is raised the banner of extreme nationalism, with the slogan of race purity, leading to errors like fascism. To incline to the left or to the right is equally dangerous. The essential thing is to lean to neither, to keep to the middle way. The true middle path of justice is the basis of Mahayana world outlook and view of human life.

Arguing about things is tedious, but Buddhism is not about anything strange to us. Its essence is simple; the perfect realization of man's "true face." The great Hideyoshi once asked Kuroda Josui: "What is the commonest thing in the world?" He replied: "A man." Then he asked him: "What is the rarest thing in the world?" He replied again: "A man." The old verse says:

Many men, but not a man among them.

O man, be a man! O man, make yourself a man!

Men can be divided into three classes: those who are necessary, those whose existence or non-existence is immaterial, and those who are better dead. Into which category do we ourselves fall, at home, in society, in the nation? For the life of Mahayana, we must do our utmost to be the first kind of man.

Then there are four types of human nature: the good, the bad, the wise, and the stupid. Those "necessary" men follow the Bodhisattva path of doing good to others and to the self also, and such are ideally wise.

He who drives the thieving sparrows *onto* his neighbour's field . . . . The wicked man.

He who drives the thieving sparrows *from* his neighbor's field . . . . The good man.

Sparrows? What sparrows? . . . The stupid man.

He who drives the sparrows from *both* fields . . . . The wise man.

When Zen master Hakuin speaks of Nirvana, he does not mean an emptiness or annihilation. It is eternal bliss, the state of satori. The pure sage rests in his own home. He whose life is worth while, a necessary man, who does his duty to others and to himself on the Bodhisattva path, is an embodiment of the ideal and has the right to Nirvana and paradise. Ah, he who has crossed beyond life-and-death, who dwells in the great bliss, how can his joy in life be told? The life of Hakuin displays it. When we see things rightly, we too can enter real life, and we have to do it.

A master has said: "When I came to pick them up, the broken tiles were gold." When the eye of the heart is opened and we see rightly, the broken stones on the road gleam with golden light. The thing is to realize the true value of the smallest fragment, the tiniest thing, that comes to us in our daily life. In Zen everything should be as far as possible simple, exact, and elegantly austere, and at all times we should treat things with reverence and not lightly. We must avoid misuse, evil use, and wrong use, and learn first *advantageous* use (and it is interesting how nowadays they are finding advantageous use even for scrap), then *loving* use, and so to *living* use, *pure* use, and finally *spiritual* use. This means to spiritualize the things as they are used. They are no longer merely things, but they are spiritual, radiating light, and then when we pick up the broken tiles they are gold. Each thing comes as a blessing, not to be wasted, and involuntarily there arise feelings of worship and reverence. This is the real religious life.

Towards the end of the last century, Tenryuji temple in Saga had for abbot the great Tekisui. When he was a young student under Abbot Gisan, he was told to bring water for the abbot's bath. He picked up the bucket and threw away a little water at the bottom before refilling it from the well.

The abbot scolded him severely for wasting life-giving water. It had such a deep effect on him that he adopted the name Tekisui, which means a drop of water, and thenceforward he did his spiritual practices in the spirit of reverence for even a drop of water. Again, Zen master Dogen, the founder of the famous Eiheiji temple, never wasted even half a cupful of water, though there was a small waterfall pouring endlessly just by the temple. From the modern point of view it seems incomprehensible, but such things had deep meaning for the spiritual training of the masters. It means not just to look at things as useful or harmful, profitable or unprofitable in the economic sense, but to penetrate into their essence and discover their spiritual use and secret virtue, to revere them for the light hidden in them. It has nothing to do with "economizing" in the worldly sense; it is recognition that the blessing must not be wasted.

When I was a child, I remember how if I spilt any rice my mother used to say: "What waste! Heaven will punish you; you will go blind!" It may be rather strong to frighten children with blindness, but anyway it is important to make them understand they should not waste even a grain of rice. Nowadays questions of education and religion are hotly debated, but the educators should first themselves realize how to use things spiritually; when in the classrooms they cease to treat a pencil simply according to its money value, but appreciate its spiritual essence, it will have a big effect on our education.

Before the Meiji Restoration, Zen master Kendo, a great spiritual figure, was abbot of the Yokenji temple of Saheki, in Kyushu. This was the temple of the Mori family, and one of their chief retainers had taken to unbridled extravagance and luxury and was sunk in a life of dissolution. The abbot, thinking it a pity, remonstrated with him a few times but instead of listening he resented the interference, and began to search for some pretext to have the abbot disgraced. The priest, however, was one of very holy life, inwardly and outwardly pure, without a single opening for criticism. But a rumour arose that every night the abbot, when the rest had gone to sleep, used to have a sumptuous repast in the privacy of his room. The retainer seized on this, and when all was dark crept into the temple garden and up to the abbot's room. He confirmed that the other was eating with apparent relish. Full of joy at having caught his enemy, he presented himself the next morning at the court of the feudal lord. The head of the Mori family was Lord Taka-yasu, a man of intelligence and furthermore a devout follower of the abbot, but when he heard the story he was taken aback, and thinking it must be true, concealed himself in the garden the next night. When he peeped into the abbot's room, sure enough the priest was eating away. Without more ado Lord Takayasu burst through the window into the room. The surprised abbot quickly covered the bowl from which he was eating and put it out of sight, then inquired: "To what urgent affair do we owe the honour of a visit at this unusual hour? Please pardon the absence of ceremony in receiving Your Grace." The Lord replied sternly: "There is no room for pardoning here. What have you just hidden away?" The abbot earnestly asked that the matter be overlooked, repeatedly excusing himself and bowing to the ground. The nobleman refused to listen and made to seize the bowl by force, upon which the abbot reluctantly showed him its contents.

He said: "I am ashamed that this should have come to the notice of Your Grace. There are many student monks who come here from different parts of the country, and though I am always impressing on them not to waste even a drop of water or throw away lightly a scrap of vegetable or grain of rice, there are so many of them, and most of them young, that in spite of all I say the cut-off ends of vegetables and rice leavings still get thrown away down the kitchen waste-pipe. To stop this waste I fixed a small sieve at the end, and when they are all asleep I collect what is in it, boil it, and have it for my own evening meal. I have been doing this now for many years. I very much regret that such a sordid story should trouble your august ears."

Hearing this, the lord was profoundly moved, and with tears in his eyes begged that his own conduct be excused. As the abbot was making his apologies, the nobleman was joining his palms and bowing before him. When I think of those two, at dead of night when the world was at rest, each bowing to the one before him and excusing his own shortcomings, I cannot restrain my tears. Today when individuals and groups and countries confront each other, they do not cast a glance at their own lack of virtue and wrong-doing, but compete in ruthlessly exposing the inadequacies and weak points of the others. How different from the picture of those two, the one great in worldly rank and the other in spiritual eminence, in mutual salutation with palms joined! Lord Takayasu took a little of the contents of the bowl, and next morning called his retainer to show it to him, relating what had happened. The latter was overcome by repentance and reformed his way of life. The change began to affect all the other members of the clan, and there arose a wave of self-imposed economy and thrift; there was a spiritual renaissance, and soon also an increase in material savings. When the Meiji Restoration came, nearly all the clans were in dire straits and did not know where to turn to meet the exigencies of the time, but this Saheki clan, though small, had the reserves to meet the emergency.

I am not urging that today we begin eating thrown away food. What we must attain is the spirit as displayed by the great abbot. This is the beginning of being able to make spiritual use of each thing. When we do not waste a drop of water or a grain of rice, we can make right use of a million gallons of water or tons of rice. When everything is spiritualized and spiritually used, the heaven of Samadhi is wide, the moon of the fourfold wisdom brilliant, and a world of infinity and light manifests.

The teaching began with "All beings are from the very beginning Buddhas," and ends with "This very body is the Buddha." After even thousands and millions of words, what after all is gained? We have to answer that nothing is gained. Shakyamuni, at the end of his forty-nine years of preaching, said that he had never uttered a word, and conversely Hakuin's sermon of no sermon, words of no words, however often repeated, are never exhausted. It is natural that in the end nothing should have been gained. But if the reader has caught even a glimpse of Hakuin's true face, he will know the meaning of the poem of the Chinese Zen poet Sotoba:

> *Mount Ro and the misty rain, and the waves in the Setsu River—*
> *Before I had been there my thousand longings never ceased.*
> *Then I went, and came back. Nothing special—*
> *Mount Ro and the misty rain, and the waves in the Setsu River!*

The misty rain on Mount Ro and the waves of the Setsu River are famous. Wishing to see them just once, after endless hopes and unbearable longing for many years, I made the journey. I saw them and returned, and—nothing special. The misty rain on Mount Ro and the river waves have not changed. The misty rain and the waves do not change, and yet before seeing and after seeing, there is a great difference. The time of longing and dreaming endlessly of them, and the time of "nothing special," when they have become part of me, are quite different.

What do we gain from seeing the true nature and attaining realization? There cannot be anything gained. As it is said: "The eyes at the sides and the nose straight in the middle; the flowers red and the willow green." No special change or marvel has come about. But the purpose of life is different. The madman runs to the east, and his keeper runs after him to the east. Equally to the east, but their purposes are different. The lunatic and the keeper look alike in that they run in the same direction, but the point of the running is quite distinct. The change in what has not changed is the real change. The real change is to change in unchanged circumstances.

The great scholar saying the same thing as an ignorant man, an expert fencer and an ordinary man walking together along a flat road—this is it. Profound is the saying that great wisdom is like stupidity, that great value is hidden deeply and looks worthless.

> *In search of flowers I went so deep into the mountains*
> *That I found myself coming out again beside a mountain*
> *village.*

When he presses on deeper and deeper, he comes out again near a human habitation. Still, the one who has gone right through the depths of the mountains and come out again is different from the one who has never gone into the deep mountains at all.

The great warrior Kumagai, after he had become a priest, was insulted and spat upon by Utsunomiya Shiro. He looked down at his priest's robe. When the other had gone, he joined his palms and made a poem:

> *The mountain is the mountain, and the path unchanged*
> *since the old days.*
> *Verily what has changed is my own heart.*

Just as the supreme good transcends good and evil, and highest beauty transcends the ugly and beautiful both, so the great realization is to transcend illusion and realization, and supreme bliss is to transcend sorrow and happiness. The great realization is that all beings are from the very beginning Buddhas, and its fulfilment is when this very place is the Lotus Paradise.

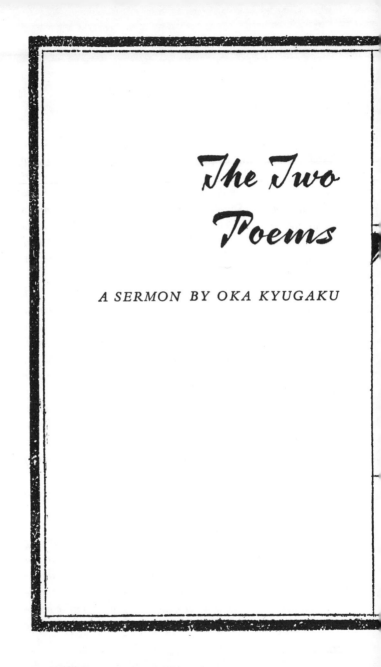

The Two Poems

A SERMON BY OKA KYUGAKU

EARLY in the sixth century A.D., Bodhidharma carried Zen to China, where he became the First Patriarch. His successors handed it on to chosen disciples. There is a tradition, not found before the time of Shumitsu, that the Fifth Patriarch invited his hundreds of disciples to submit poems from which he could judge their attainment. The head monk Jinshu wrote a verse expressing the view of gradual progress and gradual realization. Against this Eno, an obscure servant in the monastery, composed a poem on sudden realization without stages. The Fifth Patriarch approved the first poem but gave the succession to Eno, who became the Sixth Patriarch. Jinshu's school continued in the North for many years. Eno (637–713) moved to the South. The Northern school was not attacked by any of Eno's disciples except Kataku Jinne, whose own line stressed sudden realization almost to the exclusion of the traditional zazen meditation sitting. Jinne's school became purely philosophical, and with Shumitsu (779–841) became absorbed into the Kegon philosophical sect. The line of Jinne, called Kataku Zen, died out before the last remnants of the Northern school of Jinshu, which he had so bitterly attacked.

The reader is already familiar with the concept of "original realization," but an example will illustrate this difficult point. A nervous man, addicted to ghost stories, reads a well-written one late at night. He gets the notion that the ghost he has been reading about is in the house. He barricades the door; he trembles with fear and is in danger of a heart attack. In a way he knows it is all illusion, only something he has been reading about—this is his "original realization," which is never quite lost. But in practice he accepts the ghost, and this affects him physically. Every creak of the furniture and gust of wind reinforces his belief in the ghost. From the point of view of original realization there is nothing which needs to be done, as the ghost has no existence; from the point of view of practical reality, to free himself from the fear which oppresses him, he must adopt a discipline of restraining his mind from thoughts based on acceptance of the ghost's existence, and return to his original realization. But if he should regard this regimen as a sort of spell to kill the ghost, he is again asserting its existence and obscuring original realization. Even to say that the object of the practice is to free him from the ghost is not to the point; there never has been a ghost. The practice of realization is its own end. The furniture creaks and the wind blows, but the house is ever at peace.

What follows is a sermon delivered in 1930 by the famous Oka Kyugaku, late abbot of the Soto temple of Shuzenji. He was well known as an artist, and two pictures by him appear in this book.

■ *THE TWO POEMS*

IT IS SAID that the poem of the head monk Jinshu was this:
> The body is the bodhi tree,
> The heart as it were bright on the mirror-stand.
> Often and often labour to wipe it clean
> That it do not collect the dust.

It is a very fine verse. Against this, the verse of the Sixth Patriarch was:
> Bodhi is not a tree;
> The bright mirror is not on a stand.
> From the very beginning not a single thing—
> On what could the dust collect?

This verse too is very fine. Still, beginners must not think that the verse of Jinshu is bad. Of course to cling only to his idea of progress by stages is rightly condemned as a limited view, but equally to incline too much to the Sixth Patriarch's "sudden realization" will inevitably lead to spiritual pride. The Sixth Patriarch's verse is from the higher level, but spiritual students do have to polish and polish just as the verse of holy Jinshu says. An ordinary man, if he polishes enough, becomes a Buddha. It does not mean only spiritual students, but each and every one.

If a jewel is not polished, it does not shine. Even a diamond, with its innate quality of sparkling, glitters only after it has been polished. There are no ready-made Shakyamunis, no natural Mirokus. The patriarch Dogen explains: "When it is said the mind is the Buddha, it implies the quest, practice, realization, and Nirvana of all the Buddhas. Without that quest, practice, realization, and Nirvana, it is not true that the mind is the Buddha."

The practice he speaks of is zazen. Its merits are well known, but in the Zen sect zazen is itself the Buddha state. It is not that zazen is practised because we are unenlightened and that after satori zazen is not necessary. It is zazen when unenlightened and zazen also after enlightenment. Zazen is never in the expectation of satori; it is not a means with something else as an end.

If zazen is considered a means, the student may suppose that realization is somewhere else. The patriarch Dogen says on this: "Practice and realization are not different. Practice is a matter of realization. In the practice of even a novice, the original realization is fully present. It is taught that practice is to be done with care, but we are never to look for some realization apart from the practice, for practice is merely directing attention to the original realization."

Zazen itself is Buddhahood and Buddha action, and there is no point in thinking about seeking for anything else. One who is always healthy never thinks about health as such. Zazen transcends illusion and enlightenment. The patriarch says in the *Zazen-gi* meditation classic: "Do not try to make a Buddha." Real zazen transcends Buddha-making, and so it is said that the perfection of zazen is to manifest the light of the Buddhas and patriarchs. Simple people fancy this to be a light like that of the sun or moon, but he explains: "The light of sun and moon is merely an appearance in Sansara, caused by karma. The Buddha light is nothing like that. The Buddha light means receiving a text through the sense of hearing, and holding that truth by the traditional zazen. Without the Buddha light there is no holding or receiving." A phrase or a poem which contains the light of the Buddha wisdom is heard and received, and zazen means holding that Buddha light.

It is an elevating theory, yet without practice it remains only a theory. "What we must know is not the dialectics of Buddhism; instead of making distinctions in the truth, we should simply know whether our practice is real or an imitation." The real practice, namely Zen meditation, is the great life of the Buddha. Experience does not come from theorizing. When often and often we labour to polish, so that the dust does not collect, in other words when we are practising zazen, the Buddha light is seen shining.

Bodhidharma and the Emperor

FROM THE

RINZAI AND SOTO KOAN

ANTHOLOGIES

THE HEKIGANROKU *and the* Shoyoroku *are two Chinese koan anthologies, the first favoured by the Rinzai sect and the second by the Soto. The* Hekiganroku *was compiled by Setcho (979–1052) of the Ummon Zen sect, who put his own comments and poems to the hundred "cases" which he selected, and later Engo (1063–1135) of the Rinzai sect added commentaries and short ejaculatory interpolations, giving the book its present form. Similarly Wanshi (1090–1157) of the Soto sect selected and presented a hundred cases, and Bansho (1165–1246), also of the Soto, added his own comments to make the* Shoyoroku. *The Rinzai sect makes koan discipline the centre of its training, whereas in Soto Zen it is only one element, and that not indispensable.*

The case of Bodhidharma and the emperor occurs in both anthologies, and here the two presentations are put side by side so that their different flavour can be appreciated.

Emperor Bu of the Ryo dynasty was one of the great spiritual lights of Chinese Buddhism. During his long reign he built monasteries, supported their monks, and performed many other acts of Buddhist piety. When Bodhidharma came to his capital in 527, the emperor asked what merit he had gained from these actions. None, replied the patriarch. Then what, asked the bewildered emperor, is the first principle of holiness? Bodhidharma made the famous reply: "Vastness, no holiness!" When the emperor still did not understand, the teacher crossed the Yangtze River and went to Shorinji temple in the kingdom of Gi. There he sat in meditation facing a wall for nine years. After this the man appeared who became his disciple, and to whom he finally passed on the Buddha's robe and bowl, the insignia of the patriarchal succession.

The original classical Chinese prose and verse of Setcho and Wanshi is laconic and sometimes cryptic. (The remarks of the two later commentators, Engo and Bansho, tend to be too frag-mentary and allusive for readable translation, but their introduc-tions have been included.) Japanese Zen masters read these texts in the light of oral tradition and practical Zen experience. The translations which follow are based on those of an authoritative Japanese master; the rendering is not always an obvious or even likely reading of the bare Chinese original.

■ *BODHIDHARMA'S "VASTNESS!"*
　　　　　　　　　From the Hekiganroku

THE INTRODUCTION: To see smoke beyond the mountain is to know there is fire; to see a horn over the wall is to know there is an ox. From one corner displayed to know clearly the other three is only skill in inference, and to a monk an everyday affair. But when he can cut off all the streams of thought, he is free to spring up in the east or sink down in the west, to go against or with, along or across, to give or take. At that time say, of whom is this the action? Let us look at Setcho's riddle.

THE CASE: The Ryo Emperor Bu asked the teacher Bod-hidharma:

"What is the first principle of the holy truth?"

Bodhidharma said: "Vastness, no holiness!"

Quoth the emperor: "Who is it that confronts Us?"

Bodhidharma said: "Know not."

The emperor did not understand, and Bodhidharma crossed the river and went to Gi. Later the emperor asked Abbot Shiko, who said:

12. THE ZAZEN OF BODHIDHARMA, BY TAKASHINA ROSEN.
"Nine years facing the wall. Vastness, no holiness!" (See page 212.)

"Does Your Majesty yet know who is this man, or not?"

The emperor said: "(I) know not."

Shiko said: "It is the Bodhisattva Kannon, who is transmitting the seal of the Buddha heart."

The emperor in regret would have sent an envoy to ask him to return, but Shiko said:

"Though an emperor send an envoy for him, nay, though the whole people go after him, never never will he turn back."

THE HYMN:

> The holy truth is vastness—
> How to speak and hit the mark?
> "Who is it that confronts Us?"
> And he replied: "Know not."
> So in the night he crossed the river.
> How could he prevent the thorn-bushes growing after him?
> Though all the people pursue, he will not come again;
> For a thousand, ten thousand ages we are thinking after him.
> Cease from thinking. The pure breeze,
> Circling the earth, has no bounds.

Setcho looks to the left and right, and says: "Is the Patriarch here?" He replies: "He is."

"Then call him, that he may wash my feet."

■ VASTNESS, NO HOLINESS!

From the Shoyoroku

THE INTRODUCTION: In olden days Benka offered an unpolished jewel to kings, but they thought it a pebble and punished him cruelly. At night a rare gem is thrown to a man, but in alarm he clutches for his sword. An unexpected guest, but none to play the host; the borrowed virtue is not the real virtue. A priceless treasure, but he knows not what to do with it; the head of a dead cat—try him with that!

THE CASE: The Ryo emperor asked the great teacher: "What is the first principle of the holy truth?"

Bodhidharma said: "Vastness, no holiness!"

Quoth the emperor: "Who is it that confronts Us?"

Bodhidharma said: "Know not."

When the emperor did not understand, the teacher crossed the river and went to Shorinji temple: nine years facing the wall. *(Plate 12)*

THE HYMN:

Vastness, no holiness!

The moment came, but there was a gap between.

Like a master axeman, he would have cut the mud from the face but never harmed the flesh—Oh, profit!

Instead—Oh, loss! The pot smashed to the ground, but he never turned his head.

Alone, alone, he sits at Shorinji in the cold;

Silent, silent, he upholds the great tradition.

In the clear autumn sky the moon's frosty disc is wheeling;

The Milky Way pales, the stars of the Dipper hang low.

When the heir comes, he in turn will receive Robe and Bowl;

From this arises medicine but also illness for men and gods.

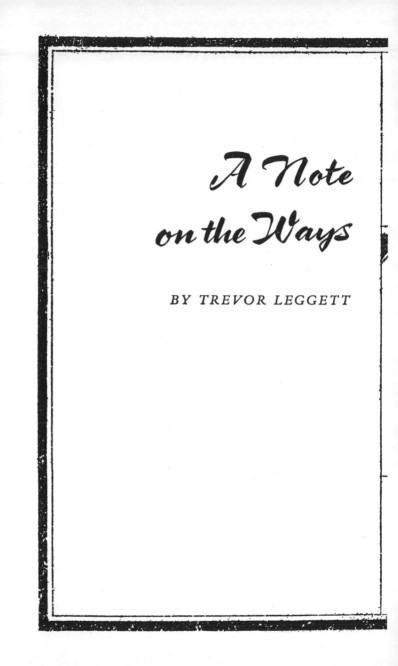

A Note
on the Ways

BY TREVOR LEGGETT

■ A NOTE ON THE WAYS

DURING the first six hundred years of Zen in China, the pupils pursued their inquiry under the teacher and meditated without being given any formal koan. Their problem would finally crystallize of itself round a phrase from a text, a spontaneous saying or gesture of the teacher, or some incident of every-day life. Later, stories of the masters of this golden age of Zen were used, especially in the Rinzai sect, to provide an artificial centre round which the pupil's energies could be concentrated almost from the beginning. When such koan become the centre of Zen practice, it is called "Kanna Zen," which means literally the Zen of seeing (into) words. The Kanna Zen masters were famous for their inspiration and joy of life; but without an expert teacher this kind of Zen can easily become an affair merely of ideas. It is not difficult to imitate the solutions given in the old stories: a shout, a laugh, a brandished fist, "the sound of the flute in the garden!" Because there is no life in such imitation, it will never deceive an expert, but it may be good enough to take in the student himself.

Japanese Buddhists had a keen spiritual intuition of the importance of relating Buddhism to daily life. Acting on hints in the Indian and Chinese traditions, they developed what are called *do* or Ways. These are fractional applications of enlightenment to arts and activities in the world. They spiritualized the arts of war such as fencing and archery, and turned the household accomplishments of flower arrangement and making tea into vehicles for spiritual inspiration.

The Ways have each two wings: first, the technical attainment without which satori will not express itself fully in the particular Way, and second, transcendence of technique and manifestation of the inspiration always radiating from the Buddha light in man.

By studying one of the Ways, the student keeps his Zen practice in touch with activity and life. If he does not receive inspiration to some extent in his chosen Way, he knows that his eye has not yet begun to open.

Going deeper and deeper into a Way, the student finds a koan or problem naturally arising. This is not something expressed in words (thereby tempting him to solve it with words), but a koan which can only be solved by inspiration in action. Success or failure is generally easy to judge, and so is overcome the worst of Zen obstacles: self-deception.

There is a body of traditional instruction on spiritual development in the Ways, most of it orally transmitted to chosen pupils only. Sometimes a *hiden* or secret transmission is passed on in writing, but mainly in the form of cryptic sentences unintelligible without an oral explanation. There are important influences in the Ways from Shingon Buddhism and from Taoism (particularly in regard to the relation of mind, body, and vitality), but most teachers would agree that a real Zen master has a perfect understanding of the essence of the Ways.

13 (opposite). EXERCISE BEFORE MEDITATION.
A monk is stretching his limbs to invigorate the body and nerves before meditation. Note the position of the fingers. This and the following three plates show pictures annexed to a Chinese text reputed to go back to Bodhidharma. It is full of Taoist terms, but some of the ideas derive from India. (See above.)

14 (page 218). CENTRES AND CURRENTS OF ENERGY.
The diagram pictures the centres and currents of vital energy along the front of the body. Reading from the bottom, they are: the Field of the Elixir *(tanden)*, the Cave of Life, the Yellow Court, the Red Palace, the Pagoda, the Magpie Bridge, and the Divine Court. In Zen and the Ways, the important preliminary point of concentration is the *tanden*. (See page 222.)

倒拽九牛尾勢

兩骸後伸

前屈

小腹運氣

空鬆

用力在於

兩膀

觀拳須注

隻瞳

坐身内功正面圖式

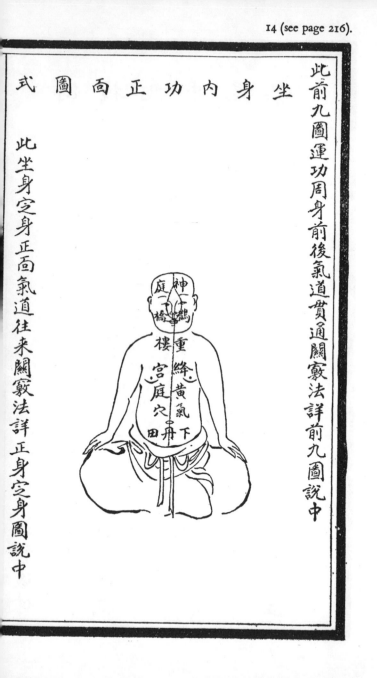

此前九圖運功周身前後氣道貫通關竅法詳前九圖說中

此坐身定身正面氣道往來關竅法詳正身定身圖說中

神庭
鵲橋
重樓
絳宮
黃庭
氣穴
下丹田

十二段錦第十二圖

十二段錦

河車搬運畢想發火燒身舊名八段錦

子後午前行勤行無間斷萬疾化為塵

背脊後頸膼後頭頂上又閉氣從額上兩太陽耳根前兩面頰

降至喉下心窩肚臍下丹田止想是發火燒通身皆熱

心想臍下丹田中

似有熱氣如火閉

氣如忍大便狀將

熱氣運至穀道即

大便處升上腰間

養嬰歸原入定出神勢

此勢坐法與定身第一

圖同但呼吸至此愈隱

愈微不惟無聲並若無

氣渾渾噩噩杳杳冥冥

一塵不染萬象皆空胎

嬰所在活活潑潑有我

無我出入悉定萬化之

原太初之本

The masters also hold that as the secret of the Ways is fundamentally one, an expert in, say, the tea ceremony will be able to understand the innermost secrets of fencing, though naturally he may not be able to express them perfectly by manipulating a sword. So far as the present writer's experience goes, this is correct. After over twenty-five years of study of the Way called judo he is more than ever conscious of the limitations of his knowledge of that Way, but he has found experts of other Ways sometimes willing to discuss and demonstrate these things, and to some extent he could understand them.

The traditional Ways are technically difficult. It is not easy to find a teacher (many teachers instruct only in technique and not in the Way); it is not easy to attain sufficient technical skill to be even considered for special training; even if skilled it is not easy to become accepted as a special pupil; it is not easy, in the final stage, to give up reliance on technical excellence.

Still, the Way is not confined to the traditional schools. If a Zen student is sufficiently alive, he can practise the Way in the simplest activities of daily life, and find in them the clue to the Samadhi of sport. In the following notes a few technical points are mentioned, but only to illustrate a general principle common to all the Ways.

15 (page 219). MEDITATION ON AN ENCLOSED FIRE.
The picture illustrates meditation on an enclosed fire at the *tanden* and afterwards along the central line of the body. This is the twelfth and last of a series of psycho-physical exercises. The artist has skilfully illustrated the atmosphere of the meditation.

16 (opposite). MEDITATION ON NURSING THE EMBRYO AND RETURNING TO THE ORIGIN.
The breath becomes soundless. In profundity and purity, where all things are the Void, there is yet the germ of life, the source of all, the root of the great Beginning. This meditation also is the culmination of a series.

THE WAY OF THE BRUSH AND THE WAY OF THE BOW: Calligraphy and archery are here taken together; each is a delicate balance of static and dynamic in a static environment. The subtlety of these arts is clearly shown in the transition from rest to movement and from movement to rest. In calligraphy a crucial moment is what is called *raku-hitsu,* when the brush comes first onto the paper for the initial stroke. The raku-hitsu is a great koan which arises to confront the ardent student of the brush *(Plates 17–18).* In archery the crucial moment is when the arrow is released, namely the passage from tension to relaxation.

In archery the question of the breath arises in a simple form, because the archer can take his time. Breathing in is represented by the sound "a" and breathing out by "um." (The two together form the diphthong "om," a very important syllable in Shingon Buddhism.) The student is made to listen to the sound of the in-breath, and to verbalize and prolong the out-breath: u-m-m-m-m-m-m-m-m. At the same time his attention is held on the tanden *(see Plate 14).* The mind is steadiest when the body is full of breath; it wavers at the change-over from out-breath to in-breath. By meditation on the tanden, the mind can be kept steady all the time. In fencing and allied arts, the ideal is to attack, when full of breath, an opponent who has just finished expiration.

Archery practised only on the range is liable to become, in the language of the Ways, "dead." Archery classics tell the student to imagine that the target is alive, that his own bow protects his body, and that his arrow is capable of splitting mighty rocks. This is an important part of the training. Japanese archers draw to the shoulder; it is more powerful but not so accurate as the Western method of drawing to the cheek or ear. A Western archer demonstrated this fact to some Japanese masters, but they remained unimpressed. When he commented on their conservatism, one of them explained that the mental training was the main thing, and

If the attention is put at the beginning of the stroke, the stroke tails off into weakness.

If the attention is put at the end of the stroke, the beginning becomes just a preliminary and shows weakness.

If we try to hold beginning *and* end together, the middle of the stroke suffers.

If we try to move the mind *with* the brush, the sense of unity is lost, and the stroke gets out of proportion (here too big).

The Koan: How to make each bit of the stroke with full attention and power, and yet keep the unity and proportion? (See opposite.)

17. THE KOAN OF THE CHINESE CHARACTER "ONE": —

suggested a duel. "If you are the better archer, you will win." The challenge was declined. There is a kindred story in a Taoist classic in which an expert archer is invited to stand beside the Taoist sage on the edge of a cliff and then shoot. He cannot do so, and the commentator adds that he does not really possess the skill unless it is with him on the cliff edge. His archery is not yet part of his life; it is not yet living in him.

In brushwork the fatal mistake is to let the brush sag in the hand, when the brushed characters become "dead." There are special methods of training to prevent this. A pupil who enrols under a teacher is shown how to hold the brush firmly. He does so for a time, and then forgets. He is told a few more times, but as he loses himself in what he is brushing, he forgets again. One day the teacher steals up behind him and snatches the brush, pulling the hairs through the pupil's hand and besmearing it with ink. It is an irritating experience, but when the pupil has washed his hands and settled down again, he is gripping the brush with instinctive firmness. Now the teacher waits a long time, but when the pupil is absorbed in a difficult stroke there may be another chance for him again to snatch the brush away. His aim is to produce a flash of anger and he does so, but the true way of gripping the brush is driven deep into the mind. The anger dies away in a short time on the reflection that the teacher is after all right, and that his only aim is the pupil's progress. No one trained in the traditional way is ever guilty of the most fatal fault, holding the brush loosely. No mere repetition could produce the same effect, nor can a pupil train himself in this way, for its essence is surprise.

KENDO, THE WAY OF THE SWORD: A samurai boy, when he entered one of the schools of martial arts, for the first months would be employed simply as a servant. Then one morning, the teacher would unexpectedly jump at him and cuff his head. "Why don't you take more care? You must not give openings for attack. If my hand had been a sword you would be dead." "Yes, master, I will take care," and the boy makes the customary bow. The teacher cuffs the bowed head. "There, again!" This time the bow would be a watchful one. Thereafter the teacher would occasionally throw a cloth or ball unexpectedly at the boy; when he could avoid them or not be disconcerted, this side of the training was approaching completion. Of course the method of training is tiring, and the pupil would rather study purely technical fencing methods for a few hours daily, and then relax and forget in his spare time. But there are many historical incidents showing that one trained by the traditional method will defeat an opponent even superior in mere technical skill.

Experts used to keep in practice, and test each other, by making mock attacks with a fan whenever an opportunity was given. The difference between technical skill and satori is illustrated in the following story: Two famous fencing masters were walking together along a mountain path. On the mountain-side above the path they saw a flower, and one said he would pick it. This was a direct challenge. He moved a boulder along the path till it was underneath the flower, then climbed onto it, stretched up, and plucked. All the time the other stood by, but the first master took great care never to give an opening or leave his companion unwatched, even when himself in the act of stretching out for the flower. He descended with it and was congratulated. They walked further and saw another flower. The flower-picker expected the other master would now attempt the same feat, but to his disappointment the latter did not notice the flower and they passed below it. Suddenly the second master was up onto a small ledge and lightly down again in one movement, with the flower in his hand. He had taken no precautions, but there had been no time to prepare an attack. As the first master stood bewildered, he received a light tap on the head from a fan, and realized he had lost twice in

18. CALLIGRAPHY BY TEACHER AND PUPIL.
(a) This is a specimen of calligraphy written by a teacher on a central line to show the balance of the characters. The *raku-hitsu* (circled) is the crucial first stroke; an expert always looks hard at this point, for it is here if anywhere that a fault will appear. *The koan:* If there is a motive for writing—profit, fame, amusement— that motive will disturb the mind, and this disturbance will be infallibly reflected in the writing. If there is no motive, how shall we begin to write? (See page 222.)

(b) This is a copy by a student of some months. It is faithful in many ways, but some of the strokes are weak. The *raku-hitsu* is surprisingly firm, until we suspect that the student has adopted a cunning means of trying to conceal his failure to solve the *raku-hitsu* problem. He has written the top left character first instead of the top right one, where the writing properly begins. He probably thought: "Perhaps the critics will overlook the weakness here." Notice the feebleness of the left-hand side of his first character. The koan has not been solved in the writer's mind.

succession. When they returned, each was asked privately his opinion of the other. The second master remarked: "He is an excellent fencer," but the first said: "I do not know by what signs to judge his attainment; he has gone beyond the fencing arts known to me. Rare indeed is such a past master."

Kendo is one of the most highly developed of the Ways; the poem of Hakuin on pages 173–74 presents its master koan, the koan of life and death.

MUSIC: Without energy and the power to concentrate that energy, no Way can be pursued. Energy is increased by living under a discipline and in association with those who know how to concentrate; it is dissipated by living planlessly and with planless people. For these and other reasons, a teacher takes certain talented pupils as residents in his home. A teacher of music, for instance, will give lessons to outside students visiting him every week; but his successor will probably be chosen from the few personal pupils in his house.

Suppose a boy is accepted as a special pupil. For some time he simply works as a servant in the house and garden. The master refuses to give him any instruction or even to notice him. The boy asks his fellow students to show him at least how to hold the instrument, but they dare not interfere. One day the senior pupil finds him in tears and listens to his entreaties. The senior says: "We students must not give you instruction; only the master can do that. However, if you are really desperate, I will try to think of something." Next time the senior conducts a beginner from outside to the master for the first weekly lesson, he leaves the sliding door a fraction open as he retires. The junior is put by the chink; it is just possible to see what is going on. Fortunately the master is speaking slowly and clearly, so that the words of instruction too can be caught. As the lesson ends the junior is whisked away, but given an old instrument with directions to practise secretly. Every week the senior makes the same arrangement. To the boy the glimpses and barely overheard words are like jewels, and he practises at every available moment. The practice hours are the most precious of his life.

After some months the master overhears him, and without any remark begins to give him formal lessons. By such methods are created the vitality and burning spirit of inquiry without which instruction is not absorbed.

JUDO: This is one of the most complicated of the Ways, and perhaps the nearest to life. It is a general training of the whole body and not concentration on a special aim with special instruments. But because of the complexity of the technique, many students become wholly absorbed in technical achievement, losing the one principle *(ri)* in study of the individual tricks *(ji)*.

In judo there is no complete rest at all; always the balance has to be actively preserved under the push and pull of the opponent. The student is expected to find the truth of the Taoist saying: "The stillness in stillness is not the real stillness; only when there is stillness in movement does the universal rhythm manifest."

In Plate 19 the attacker (on the right) finds a small chance and comes in. At the crucial moment the opponent will either shift his right foot forward to take his weight, or keep it still (steps 2 or 6). If he moves his right foot, then the throw in the left-hand column (A) will succeed, and the one in the right-hand column (B) fails; if he does not move, then B will succeed and A will fail. The difficulty is that if we wait to see which he will do, we shall hesitate, and the rhythm of the movement will be lost. (The complete whirling action in B takes only about a second.) If we do not hesitate but go in blindly, we are liable to find ourselves attempting the wrong throw.

As in most of these koan, there is a sort of cheating

A

1. Attacker (on right) is about to swing his left leg forward.

2. If opponent braces his right leg by stepping forward . . .

3. attacker takes his left foot forward and plants it down . . .

4. swings his right leg through . . .

5. and throws opponent to the *rear*.

B

6. If opponent leaves his right foot where it is . . .

7. attacker swings his left leg in front . . .

8. whirls his body round and down . . .

9. and throws opponent to the *front*.

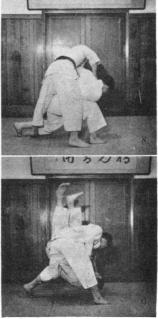

The koan: If you anticipate one alternative, but he takes the other, the throw is blocked. If you wait to see what he does, you hesitate and spoil the throwing action. If you make your mind a blank, your body will not move. How to solve the problem? (See page 229.)

20. NO HOLDING BACK.

This winning throw from an important contest is a wonderful feat of technique. The strong resisting opponent, himself an expert, is carried high into the air by the *tori*, Mr. Watanabe Kisaburo, the combined weight being balanced on the toe-tips of the left foot. Apart from technical difficulties, beginners for a long time hesitate to throw the body into the attack, taking the head right down. They have to screw themselves up to it and so lose the opportunity, which is very short. The Zen sayings are "Enter at one stroke" and "Throw away the body to find the spirit." (See page 233.)

method by which we can half solve the problem. Suppose we have tried B and succeeded; when we come in again in the same way, the other man will probably expect B again, and this time he will move his right foot. If we have anticipated this, we can go smoothly into the other throw. Then next time we change again. Simple alternation is of course too obvious for success, but good results can be obtained by determining in advance a sequence like A-B-A-A-A or A-B-B-B-A and so on. Still the problem is not solved. By determining our action in advance we get the advantage of smooth uninterrupted movement, but often we shall still be trying the wrong throw and be doomed to fail.

There is a song of the Way on the point:

The trees on the mountain are not so thick
That from time to time a moonbeam
Cannot penetrate.

Perhaps we can find an intellectual application of this verse to the problem, but unless it can help us to find a solution in practice, we cannot be said to understand it. *(See Plate 20.)*

SWEEPING: Students of the Ways are expected to find opportunities to practise when engaged in household activities. Before beginning to sweep the floor or garden, a pupil may be told to press his finger between the brows and then bring it down the central line of the body to a point just below the navel (tanden). When the finger is removed, for a short time the sensation of pressure remains, and the beginner uses that as the basis for bringing his attention to the central line. Then he meditates that it is a line of light, and the rest of the body becomes shadowy and empty. Now he begins sweeping with the broom, but keeping up the meditation on the central line.

After some weeks the student can maintain the attention on the central line for longer than a minute or two. He does not need to use the finger pressure at the beginning. When the mind wanders off he brings it back. Meditation in this way relaxes the nerves and has an effect on posture and on movement, making the latter more efficient. An expert can tell by looking at the movement whether the pupil's mind has remained on the line or been distracted.

TYPING: Part of the day the typist must practise perfect typing, reducing errors until the copy is perfect. This is the technical side. When substantial progress has been made on that side, the pupil may sometimes practise the line of light meditation while typing. All desires, fears, will, and body attachment must be relaxed. Will not the typing come to a full stop if the desires and will are abandoned? This is the koan, and it is solved by actual practice and not by words.

In everyday activities such as typing can be found hints for the solution of many Zen puzzles. "What is Buddhism?" "I don't know," replies the master. Then how can he be an enlightened man? The unenlightened man does not know, and if the master also does not know, what is the difference between them?

Consider the man who cannot type at all. He does not know the position of the letters and figures on the keyboard. He does not know, and he cannot type. Now take the learner. He painfully memorizes the rows of keys: A for the little finger of the left hand, S for the next finger, D for the middle finger, F and also G for the index finger. And so on, gradually learning the whole keyboard. He is one who knows, but he still cannot type very well, because he must constantly refer to his memorized plan of the keys. Finally, look at the expert touch typist. He has quite forgotten the position of the letters, and if asked suddenly what are the keys next to J he says: "I don't know." He does not know, but he types perfectly. Of him we cannot really say he does know, but neither is it quite true to say he does not know. He more than knows; it has become part of him.

In the same way the "know not" of Bodhidharma is

different from the "know not" of the emperor. Bodhi-dharma in his every action expresses the knowledge which is more-than-knowledge; he does not know it as an intellectual idea any more, and those intellectual ideas are a nuisance and would hamper his free expression if he harboured them. But at one time he had them and then they were not useless as steps on the Way. It is the same with Zen and scriptural learning.

CHESS: A young man who had a bitter disappointment in life went to a remote monastery and said to the abbot: "I am disillusioned with life and wish to attain enlightenment to be freed from these sufferings. But I have no capacity for sticking long at anything. I could never do long years of meditation and study and austerity; I should relapse and be drawn back to the world again, painful though I know it to be. Is there any short way for people like me?" "There is," said the abbot, "if you are really determined. Tell me, what have you studied, what have you concentrated on most in your life?" "Why, nothing really. We were rich, and I did not have to work. I suppose the thing I was really interested in was chess. I spent most of my time at that."

The abbot thought for a moment, and then said to his attendant: "Call such-and-such a monk, and tell him to bring a chessboard and men." The monk came with the board and the abbot set up the men. He sent for a sword and showed it to the two. "O monk," he said, "you have vowed obedience to me as your abbot, and now I require it of you. You will play a game of chess with this youth, and if you lose I shall cut off your head with this sword. But I promise that you will be reborn in paradise. If you win, I shall cut off the head of this man; chess is the only thing he has ever tried hard at, and if he loses he deserves to lose his head also." They looked at the abbot's face and saw that he meant it: he would cut off the head of the loser.

They began to play. With the opening moves the youth

felt the sweat trickling down to his heels as he played for his life. The chessboard became the whole world; he was entirely concentrated on it. At first he had somewhat the worst of it, but then the other made an inferior move and he seized his chance to launch a strong attack. As his opponent's position crumbled, he looked covertly at him. He saw a face of intelligence and sincerity, worn with years of austerity and effort. He thought of his own worthless life, and a wave of compassion came over him. He deliberately made a blunder and then another blunder, ruining his position and leaving himself defenceless.

The abbot suddenly leant forward and upset the board. The two contestants sat stupefied. "There is no winner and no loser," said the abbot slowly, "there is no head to fall here. Only two things are required," and he turned to the young man, "complete concentration, and compassion. You have today learnt them both. You were completely concentrated on the game, but then in that concentration you could feel compassion and sacrifice your life for it. Now stay here a few months and pursue our training in this spirit and your enlightenment is sure." He did so and got it.